THOMPSON IS IN TROUBLE, CHARLIE BROWN

Books by Charles M. Schulz

Peanuts
More Peanuts
Good Grief, More Peanuts!
Good Ol' Charlie Brown
Snoopy
You're Out of Your Mind, Charlie Brown!
But We Love You, Charlie Brown
Peanuts Revisited
Go Fly a Kite, Charlie Brown
Peanuts Every Sunday
It's a Dog's Life, Charlie Brown
You Can't Win, Charlie Brown
Snoopy, Come Home
You Can Do It, Charlie Brown
We're Right Behind You, Charlie Brown
As You Like It, Charlie Brown
Sunday's Fun Day, Charlie Brown
You Need Help, Charlie Brown
Snoopy and the Red Baron
The Unsinkable Charlie Brown
You'll Flip, Charlie Brown
You're Something Else, Charlie Brown
Peanuts Treasury
You're You, Charlie Brown
You've Had It, Charlie Brown
Snoopy and His Sopwith Camel
A Boy Named Charlie Brown
You're Out of Sight, Charlie Brown
Peanuts Classics
You've Come a Long Way, Charlie Brown
Snoopy and "It Was a Dark and Stormy Night"
"Ha Ha, Herman," Charlie Brown
The "Snoopy, Come Home" Movie Book
Snoopy's Grand Slam
Thompson Is in Trouble, Charlie Brown

THOMPSON IS IN TROUBLE, CHARLIE BROWN

A NEW *PEANUTS*® BOOK

by Charles M. Schulz

HOLT, RINEHART AND WINSTON
New York • Chicago • San Francisco

Published simultaneously in Canada by Holt, Rinehart and Winston of Canada, Limited.

First published in book form in 1973.

ISBN: 0-03-007741-9

Library of Congress Catalog Card Number: 72-91589

First Edition

Printed in the United States of America

WHAT ARE YOU READING, FRANKLIN?
IT'S A BOOK ON PSYCHOLOGY.. FROM WHAT I UNDERSTAND, IT SEEMS TO BE PRETTY GOOD..
FORGET IT, FRANKLIN...
NO BOOK ON PSYCHOLOGY CAN BE ANY GOOD IF ONE CAN UNDERSTAND IT!
SCHULZ

This is my theme on Memorial Day which I am writing on Monday because there is no school today.
Everyone is observing Memorial Day today so they can have a three-day weekend and go water skiing.
Which hasn't much to do with Memorial Day which is really tomorrow.
THIS IS THE SORT THEME WHERE YOU GET EITHER AN "A" OR AN "F"!
SCHULZ

LISTEN...OUR NEW BABY BROTHER IS CRYING
FOR A LONG WHILE YOU HAD JUST ONE BABY BROTHER..
SUDDENLY, YOU HAVE TWO!
AT THIS TIME OF THE YEAR ALL YOU EVER GET IS RERUNS!
SCHULZ

AT FIRST, I WANTED TO BE AN ONLY CHILD
YOU SPOILED THAT! THEN I THOUGHT MAYBE IT WOULD BE KIND OF NICE TO HAVE A SISTER.. SO WHAT HAPPENS? I GET ANOTHER BROTHER..A RERUN!
THAT'S IT!
WE'LL CALL HIM "RERUN"!
"RERUN" VAN PELT... GOOD GRIEF!
SCHULZ

"RERUN" IS CRYING AGAIN I CAN HEAR HIM...
WHEN BABIES ARE HUNGRY, THEY DON'T WANT TO WAIT
IT TAKES A LONG TIME TO LEARN PATIENCE..
BUMP!
SOME PEOPLE I KNOW NEVER LEARN ANY PATIENCE!
I'M VERY PATIENT...IT'S MY STOMACH THAT'S CRABBY!
SCHULZ

"HUNDREDS OF PIRATES SWARMED ABOARD THE SHIP"
"THE CABIN BOY WAS WOUNDED SO HE PLAYED POSSUM"
WHEN A PERSON PRETENDS THAT HE'S DEAD, WE CALL IT "PLAYING POSSUM"
PIRATE STORIES
WHAT DO THE POSSUMS CALL IT ?
SCHULZ

Z
BONK!
Z
Z
KLUNK!
Z
Z
Z
Z
KLUNK!
Z
KLUNK!
Z
Z
KLUNK
KLUNK
KLUNK
KLUNK
KLUNK
KLUNK
KLUNK
ALL THE WAY INTO THE BASEMENT!
SCHULZ

HAPPY
DAY!
WHAT ARE YOU DOING?
I'M MAKING SORT OF A FATHER'S DAY CARD
THAT'S GREAT! I'M PROUD OF YOU! FATHER'S DAY DOESN'T GET THE RECOGNITION IT DESERVES...
I FIND THAT IT IS ALL TOO FREQUENTLY IGNORED...
I CANNOT COMMEND YOU TOO HIGHLY...I'M VERY IMPRESSED..
THANK YOU
DEAR MOM - HAVE A HAPPY FATHER'S DAY!
SCHULZ

SCHOOL IS OUT!
NO MORE SCHOOL! SCHOOL IS OUT!!
ALL RIGHT, EVERYONE OVER HERE FOR THE CAMP BUS! IN YOU GO! HURRY IT UP! EVERYONE TO SUMMER CAMP!
WHATEVER HAPPENED TO GOING HOME?
SCHULZ

LOOK AT THIS CAMP...RIGHT OUT IN THE WOODS!
I'LL BET THIS PLACE IS FILLED WITH GULLY CATS JUST WAITING TO BITE A PERSON ON THE ARM
ON THE ARM?
GULLY CATS KNOW THAT TENNIS RACKETS ARE MADE WITH GULLY CAT GUT...
THEY LIKE TO BITE PEOPLE ON THE ARM SO THEY CAN'T PLAY TENNIS ANY MORE!
MAYBE WE COULD GET THEM TO THINK NYLON
SCHULZ

CHARLIE BROWN, I HAVE A QUESTION..
HOW COME WE END UP AT SUMMER CAMP EVERY YEAR WHEN WE REALLY DON'T WANT TO GO?
I THINK IT'S JUST SOMETHING THAT HAPPENS TO CITY KIDS...
IT'S CALLED URBAN RENEWAL
SCHULZ

GOLLY, SIR, IT'S GREAT TO SEE YOU AT CAMP AGAIN THIS YEAR
STOP CALLING ME "SIR"!
DO YOU REMEMBER ME? MY NAME IS MARCIE.. WE WERE IN THE SAME TENT LAST YEAR
OF COURSE, I REMEMBER YOU...
AS SOON AS I SAW YOU GET OFF THE BUS, I SAID, "WELL, IF IT ISN'T WHAT'S-HER-FACE!"
I APPRECIATE YOUR REMEMBERING ME, SIR...
STOP CALLING ME "SIR"!
SCHULZ

ARE WE GOING AROUND THE LAKE THIS YEAR, AND VISIT THE BOYS' CAMP, SIR?
I DON'T KNOW...MAYBE WE SHOULD JUST STAY HERE, AND SEE IF THEY VISIT US...
IT'S A LONG DAY, AND IT'S A BIG LAKE..
AND LIFE IS TOO SHORT... LET'S GO!!
I LIKE YOUR WAY OF THINKING, SIR!
STOP CALLING ME "SIR"!
SCHULZ

I CAN HARDLY WAIT TO SEE OL' CHUCK...WE'RE GONNA HAVE A GREAT TIME!
SIR, I DIDN'T TELL YOU, DID I, BUT THERE'S ANOTHER GIRL IN OUR CAMP WHO KNOWS CHUCK..
ANOTHER GIRL? WHO?
I DON'T KNOW HER NAME, BUT SHE HAS RED HAIR, AND SHE SAID SHE USED TO GO TO THE SAME SCHOOL WITH CHUCK...
SIR, WHY ARE YOU STANDING WITH YOUR HEAD AGAINST THAT TREE?
SCHULZ

LET ME GET THIS STRAIGHT..YOU MEAN THAT RED-HAIRED GIRL CHUCK ALWAYS TALKS ABOUT IS IN **OUR** CAMP?
SHE SAID SHE USED TO GO TO SCHOOL WITH HIM...
LET'S GO BACK.. I WANT TO HAVE A TALK WITH HER..
WHAT ARE YOU LOOKING AT, LINUS?
THOSE TWO GIRLS DOWN THERE..THEY WERE WALKING AROUND THE LAKE..
THEY WERE COMING THIS WAY...THEN, THEY STOPPED, AND SUDDENLY TURNED AROUND AND RAN BACK!
I HATE MYSTERIES
SCHULZ

ALL RIGHT, WHERE IS SHE? POINT OUT THE RED-HAIRED GIRL TO ME...
YOU'RE STILL IN LOVE WITH CHUCK, AREN'T YOU, SIR?
STOP CALLING ME "SIR"! ALL I WANT TO DO IS MEET THIS GIRL CHUCK IS ALWAYS TALKING ABOUT!
SLUGGING HER WON'T SOLVE ANYTHING, SIR...
IF YOU DON'T HURRY UP, AND POINT HER OUT TO ME, I'M GONNA SLUG **YOU**!
I'M NOT AFRAID OF YOU, SIR!
AAUGH!
SCHULZ

THERE SHE IS, SIR! THERE'S THE LITTLE RED-HAIRED GIRL!
SHE SAID SHE USED TO GO TO SCHOOL WITH CHUCK..ARE YOU GOING TO TALK TO HER? ARE YOU GOING TO HIT HER? WHAT ARE YOU GOING TO DO? SIR? SIR?
WHAT ARE YOU LOOKING AT NOW, LINUS?
THERE SEEMS TO BE SOME EXCITEMENT IN THE GIRLS' CAMP..
WHAT DO YOU THINK IT COULD BE?
ONE OF THEM PROBABLY SAW A QUEEN SNAKE...
SCHULZ

HEY, KID...IS YOUR NAME BROWN? YOU'RE WANTED AT THE COUNSELOR'S OFFICE!
ME?
ME? WHY ME? WHY WOULD THE COUNSELOR WANT ME? MAYBE THEY'RE GOING TO PUT ME TO WORK IN THE KITCHEN..MAYBE I'LL HAVE TO CLEAN OUT THE GREASE TRAP
I HOPE I DON'T HAVE TO CLEAN OUT THE GREASE TRAP.. MAYBE THEY WON'T EVEN THINK ABOUT IT...
GOOD EVENING, SIR...HOW'S THE GREASE TRAP?
SCHULZ

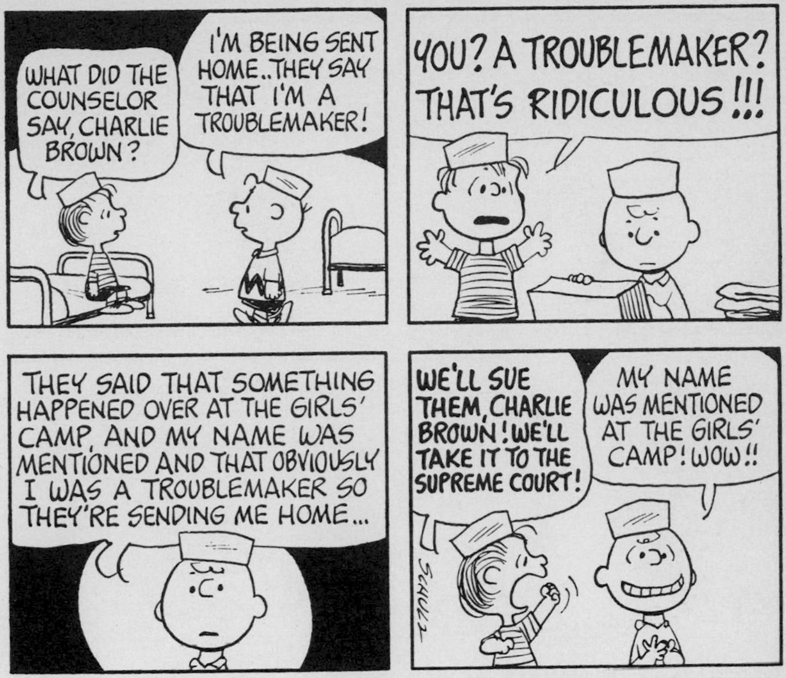
WHAT DID THE COUNSELOR SAY, CHARLIE BROWN?
I'M BEING SENT HOME..THEY SAY THAT I'M A TROUBLEMAKER!
YOU? A TROUBLEMAKER? THAT'S RIDICULOUS!!!
THEY SAID THAT SOMETHING HAPPENED OVER AT THE GIRLS' CAMP, AND MY NAME WAS MENTIONED AND THAT OBVIOUSLY I WAS A TROUBLEMAKER SO THEY'RE SENDING ME HOME...
WE'LL SUE THEM, CHARLIE BROWN! WE'LL TAKE IT TO THE SUPREME COURT!
MY NAME WAS MENTIONED AT THE GIRLS' CAMP! WOW!!
SCHULZ

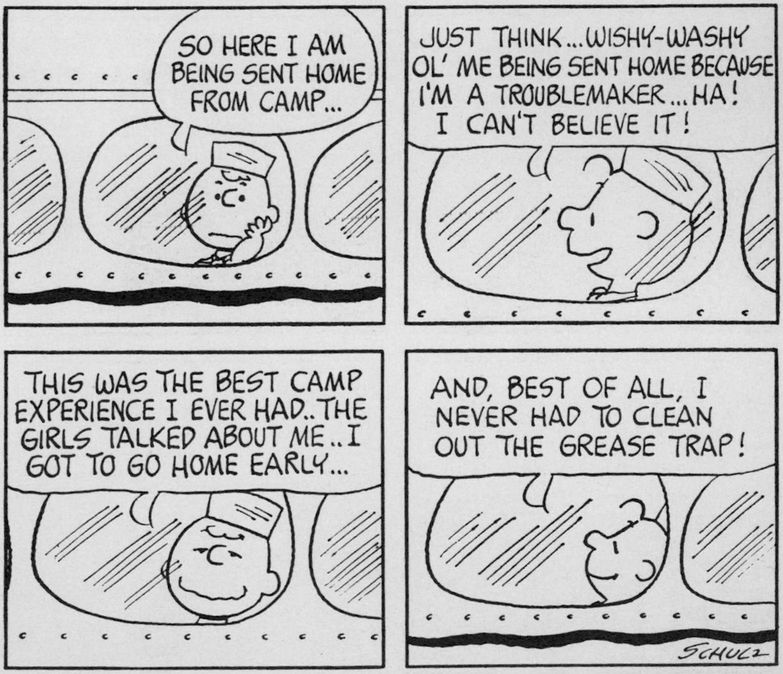
SO HERE I AM BEING SENT HOME FROM CAMP...
JUST THINK...WISHY-WASHY OL' ME BEING SENT HOME BECAUSE I'M A TROUBLEMAKER...HA! I CAN'T BELIEVE IT!
THIS WAS THE BEST CAMP EXPERIENCE I EVER HAD..THE GIRLS TALKED ABOUT ME..I GOT TO GO HOME EARLY...
AND, BEST OF ALL, I NEVER HAD TO CLEAN OUT THE GREASE TRAP!
SCHULZ

HI, SNOOPY.. I JUST GOT HOME FROM CAMP...
IT'S GOOD TO SEE YOU AGAIN
MERCI, MON AMI !
JOE FRENCH !

PEPPERMINT PATTY! WHAT ARE YOU DOING HERE?
WORKING ON MY GUILT FEELINGS..WHERE'S CHUCK? I HAVE TO SEE HIM..
THEY SENT HIM HOME..THEY SAID HE WAS THE CAUSE OF SOME TROUBLE IN THE GIRLS' CAMP..
I'M THE TROUBLE, LINUS! IT WAS ALL MY FAULT! I FEEL TERRIBLE...
I THINK I'M GETTING SICK... I FEEL SHAKY..
HERE, HOLD THIS FOR AWHILE.. IT'LL CALM YOU DOWN...
Z
GUT-LEVEL MEDICINE!

WHAT HAPPENED AT THE GIRLS' CAMP, PATTY?
I SAW THE LITTLE RED-HAIRED GIRL, LINUS...
I HEARD THAT SOMEONE GOT QUITE UPSET... WHAT HAPPENED?
I ACTUALLY SAW HER, LINUS...
I STOOD RIGHT IN FRONT OF HER...I FINALLY SAW THE LITTLE RED-HAIRED GIRL THAT CHUCK IS ALWAYS TALKING ABOUT.. AND YOU KNOW WHAT I DID?
I CRIED, LINUS..I CRIED AND CRIED AND CRIED!
YOU'D BETTER GIVE ME MY BLANKET BACK... I DON'T THINK I'M READY FOR THIS...
SCHULZ

I STOOD IN FRONT OF THAT LITTLE RED-HAIRED GIRL AND I SAW HOW PRETTY SHE WAS...
SUDDENLY, I REALIZED WHY CHUCK HAS ALWAYS LOVED HER, AND I REALIZED THAT NO ONE WOULD EVER LOVE ME THAT WAY..
I STARTED TO CRY, AND I COULDN'T STOP...I MADE A FOOL OUT OF MYSELF, BUT I DIDN'T CARE! I JUST LOOKED AT HER AND I CRIED AND CRIED AND CRIED...
I HAVE A BIG NOSE AND MY SPLIT-ENDS HAVE SPLIT-ENDS, AND I'LL ALWAYS BE FUNNY-LOOKING, AND I THINK I'M GOING TO CRY AGAIN.........
SCHULZ

I LOOKED AT THAT LITTLE RED HAIRED GIRL, LINUS, AND I STARTED TO CRY AND I COULDN'T STOP..
SHE'S SO PRETTY..SHE JUST SORT OF SPARKLES..I'LL NEVER SPARKLE..I'M A MUD FENCE..I'M A PLAIN JANE...I FEEL LIKE THE GIRL WHO WANTED TO GO INTO THE BACK YARD AND EAT WORMS...
THE ONLY PERSON WHO EVER KNOWS HOW I FEEL IS SNOOPY.. IF SNOOPY WERE HERE, HE'D LEAN OVER AND KISS ME ON THE CHEEK..
SMAK!
LIKE THIS, SWEETIE?
SCHULZ

YOU KISSED ME, LINUS!
'BEAUTY IS IN THE EYE OF THE BEHOLDER,' PATTY..
SOMEDAY, SOMEONE IS GOING TO LOOK AT YOU AND SAY, "BEHOLD! A GREAT BEAUTY!"
SIR, THE BUS FOR HOME IS LEAVING IN AN HOUR..
LINUS JUST KISSED ME ON THE CHEEK, AND YOU TELL ME THE BUS IS LEAVING!
NEVER TAKE A SUMMER ROMANCE SERIOUSLY, SIR..
STOP CALLING ME "SIR"!!
SCHULZ

Now is the time for all foxes to jump over the lazy dog.
SOMEHOW, THAT DOESN'T SEEM QUITE RIGHT...
SCHULZ

WHAT A GREAT TITLE FOR MY NEW BOOK...
"THINGS I'VE LEARNED AFTER IT WAS TOO LATE"
SCHULZ

Things I've Learned After It Was Too Late
Never argue with the cat next door. He's always right
SCHULZ

Things I've Learned After It Was Too late.
A whole stack of memories will never equal one little hope.
I KIND OF LIKE THAT
SCHULZ

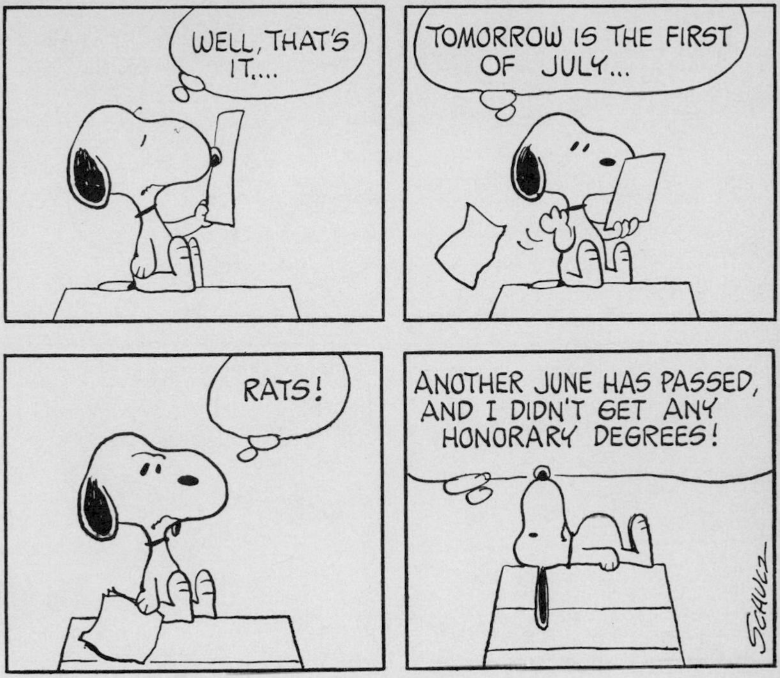
WELL, THAT'S IT....
TOMORROW IS THE FIRST OF JULY...
RATS!
ANOTHER JUNE HAS PASSED, AND I DIDN'T GET ANY HONORARY DEGREES!
SCHULZ

WELL, HOW DO YOU LIKE HAVING A NEW BABY BROTHER?
OH, "RERUN" IS ALL RIGHT, I GUESS...ACTUALLY, I'D ALWAYS HOPED TO BE AN ONLY CHILD, BUT IT'S TOO LATE FOR THAT NOW...
MAYBE IT'LL BE DIFFERENT WHEN YOU ALL GROW UP... MAYBE YOU'LL BECOME REAL CLOSE...
JOE FAMILY!
SCHULZ

"MOST COWBOYS WERE EXCELLENT RIDERS.."
Tales of the West
"GALLOPING ACROSS THE PRAIRIE WAS FUN, BUT IT COULD ALSO BE DANGEROUS.."
"A HORSE COULD VERY EASILY STUMBLE IF HE STEPPED INTO A HOLE.."
WOULDN'T IT HAVE BEEN SAFER JUST TO STAY ON THE SIDEWALK?
SCHULZ

Today is the Fourth of July.
This holiday is a celebration of freedom. It all began when
SCHOOL IS OUT..YOU DON'T HAVE TO WRITE THEMES ABOUT HOLIDAYS WHEN SCHOOL IS OUT...
I'M A VICTIM OF PROGRAMMING
SCHULZ

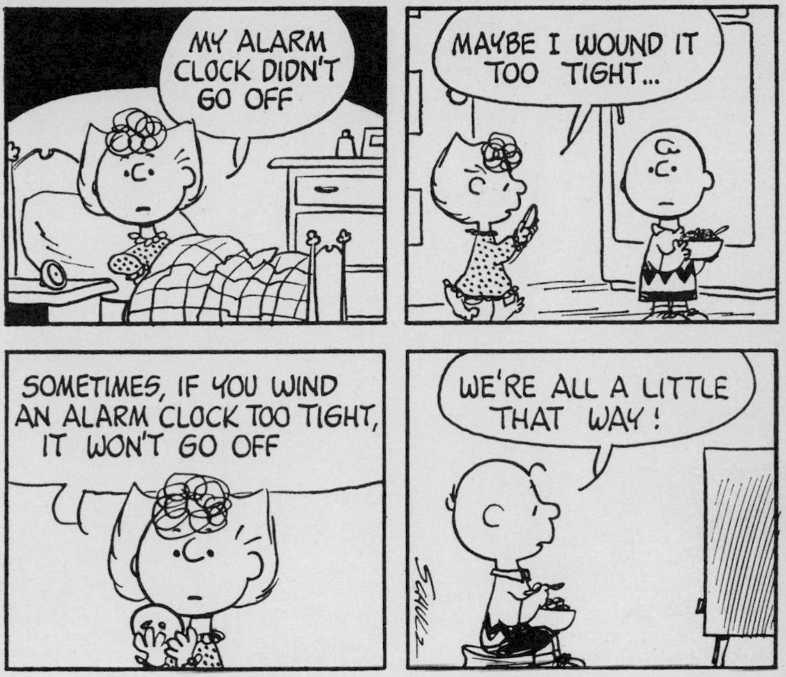
MY ALARM CLOCK DIDN'T GO OFF
MAYBE I WOUND IT TOO TIGHT...
SOMETIMES, IF YOU WIND AN ALARM CLOCK TOO TIGHT, IT WON'T GO OFF
WE'RE ALL A LITTLE THAT WAY!

THANK YOU... I'LL TRY TO DO WHAT YOU SUGGESTED
CHARLIE BROWN JUST GAVE ME SOME ADVICE...
DID YOU UNDERSTAND IT?
OF COURSE, I UNDERSTOOD IT!
NEVER TAKE ANY ADVICE THAT YOU CAN UNDERSTAND... IT CAN'T POSSIBLY BE ANY GOOD!

STRIKE TWO!
STRIKE THREE!
RATS!
I'LL NEVER BE A BIG-LEAGUE PLAYER! I JUST DON'T HAVE IT! ALL MY LIFE I'VE DREAMED OF PLAYING IN THE BIG LEAGUES, BUT I KNOW I'LL NEVER MAKE IT...
YOU'RE THINKING TOO FAR AHEAD, CHARLIE BROWN...WHAT YOU NEED TO DO IS TO SET YOURSELF MORE IMMEDIATE GOALS...
IMMEDIATE GOALS?
YES
START WITH THIS NEXT INNING WHEN YOU GO OUT TO PITCH..
SEE IF YOU CAN WALK OUT TO THE MOUND WITHOUT FALLING DOWN!
SCHULZ

WOODSTOCK LIKES TO LISTEN TO MY STEREO..
"AMERICAN PIE" OVER AND OVER AND OVER AND OVER...
SCHULZ

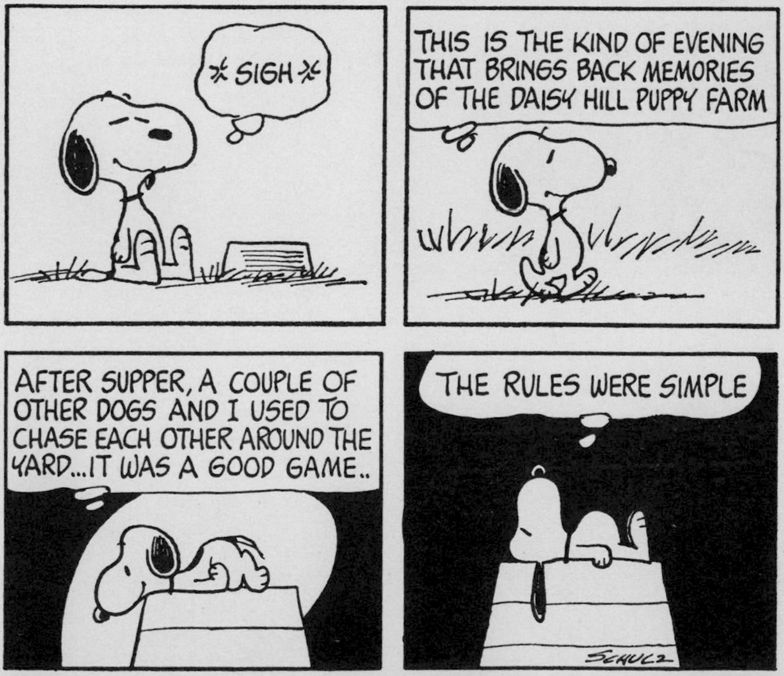
* SIGH *
THIS IS THE KIND OF EVENING THAT BRINGS BACK MEMORIES OF THE DAISY HILL PUPPY FARM
AFTER SUPPER, A COUPLE OF OTHER DOGS AND I USED TO CHASE EACH OTHER AROUND THE YARD...IT WAS A GOOD GAME..
THE RULES WERE SIMPLE
SCHULZ

I DON'T UNDERSTAND WHY YOU STAY UP THERE IN THE HOT SUN..
YOU'D BE MUCH COOLER SLEEPING OVER THERE UNDERNEATH THAT TREE
I NEVER SLEEP UNDERNEATH A TREE..
THAT'S A GOOD WAY TO GET HOPPED ON BY A HEDGE TOAD!
SCHULZ

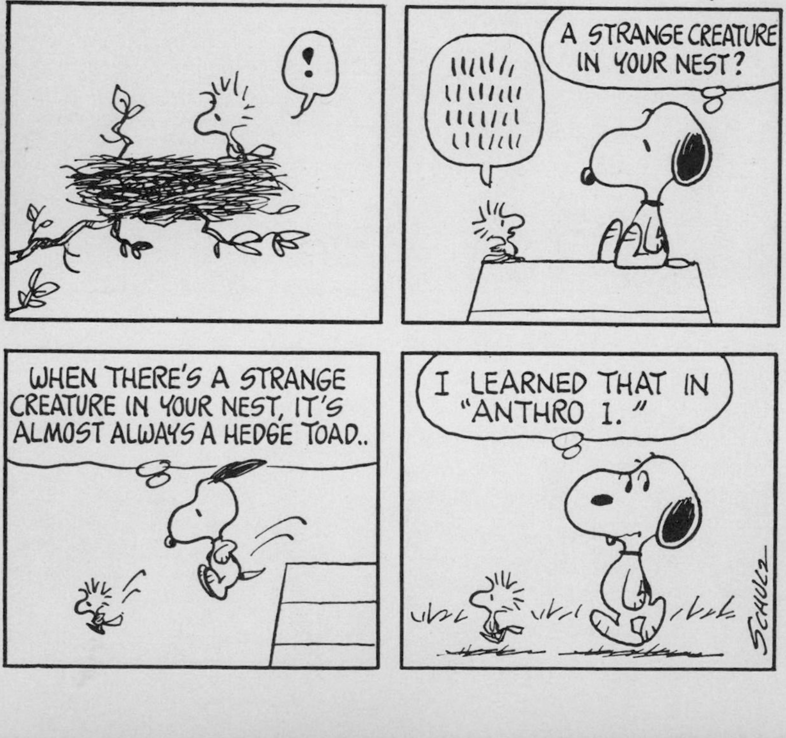
!
A STRANGE CREATURE IN YOUR NEST?
WHEN THERE'S A STRANGE CREATURE IN YOUR NEST, IT'S ALMOST ALWAYS A HEDGE TOAD..
I LEARNED THAT IN "ANTHRO I."
SCHULZ

WOODSTOCK SAYS THERE'S A STRANGE CREATURE IN HIS NEST..
I'LL BET I COULD CLIMB THAT TREE IF SOMEONE GAVE ME A BOOST...
THEN AGAIN, MAYBE THERE'S A BETTER WAY..
SIGH
SCHULZ

IF YOU CAN'T CLIMB A TREE, THE OBVIOUS THING TO DO IS TO GET A LADDER..
SCHULZ

A STRANGE CREATURE IN WOODSTOCK'S NEST?
MAYBE IT'S A HEDGE TOAD..
THAT'S JUST WHAT I WAS THINKING
I HAVE A BOOK AT HOME THAT TELLS ALL ABOUT SUCH STRANGE CREATURES...I'LL GO GET IT...
HERE IT IS... IT'S CALLED "HEDGE TOADS, QUEEN SNAKES AND GULLY CATS"
I HAVEN'T READ THE BOOK, BUT I READ SOME OF THE REVIEWS

IT LOOKS LIKE WE'RE GOING TO HAVE TO CLIMB THE TREE...
THE ONLY WAY TO FIND OUT WHO'S IN WOODSTOCK'S NEST IS TO CLIMB THIS TREE AND SEE FOR OURSELVES...
SO IF YOU'LL GIVE ME A LITTLE BOOST, AND WOODSTOCK GIVES YOU A LITTLE BOOST, I THINK WE CAN DO IT...
OKAY... BOOST!
I'M BOOSTING! BUT I'M NOT SURE IF MY BOOSTER IS BOOSTING!

WE'RE GETTING THERE, SNOOPY!
WE'RE GOING TO CLIMB THIS TREE, AND FIND OUT WHO'S IN WOODSTOCK'S NEST...
WE MADE IT! I'M AT THE TOP OF THE TREE!
IF THIS IS THE TOP OF THE TREE, WHY IS THE SKY GREEN?
SCHULZ

SNOOPY!
SNOOPY?
DO YOU SEE WOODSTOCK'S NEST?
WHERE ARE YOU?
SNOOPY?
SNOOPY?!
HOW CAN ANYONE GET LOST IN A TREE?
SCHULZ

WHAT ARE YOU DOING UP IN THAT TREE?
LOOKING FOR SOMETHING... CAN YOU SEE SNOOPY? WE CLIMBED UP HERE TOGETHER, BUT NOW I DON'T SEE HIM...
BEAGLES CAN'T CLIMB TREES..
YOU'RE RIGHT!
KLUNK!
SCHULZ

YOU STUPID BEAGLE, WHAT ARE YOU DOING CLIMBING AROUND IN A TREE?
DON'T YELL AT HIM... WE'RE TRYING TO FIND A "STRANGE CREATURE" IN A NEST...
YOU'RE BOTH CRAZY! GO AHEAD AND KNOCK YOURSELVES OUT! I COULDN'T CARE LESS!!
RATS...I WAS HOPING FOR A HUG!
SCHULZ

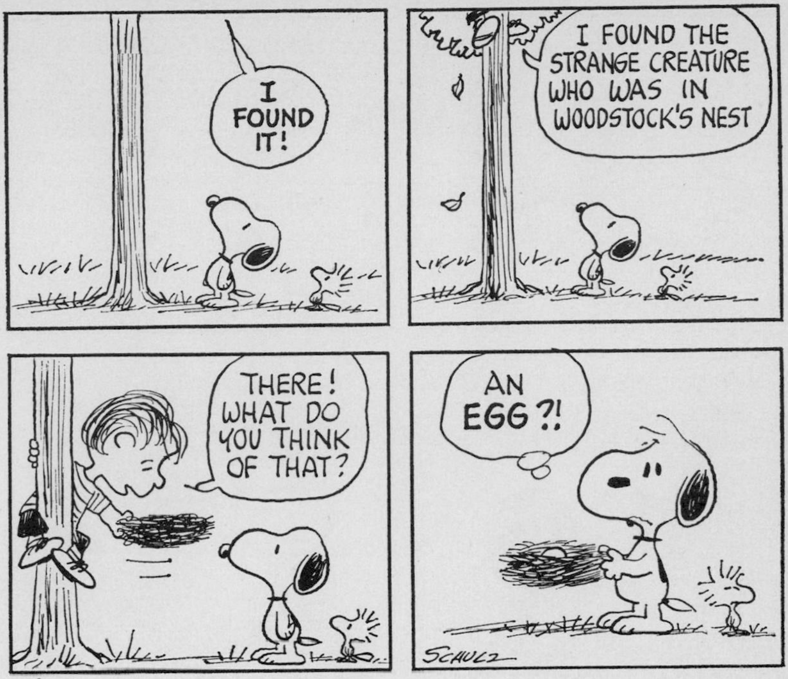
I FOUND IT!
I FOUND THE STRANGE CREATURE WHO WAS IN WOODSTOCK'S NEST
THERE! WHAT DO YOU THINK OF THAT?
AN EGG?!
SCHULZ

THIS IS THE "STRANGE CREATURE" THAT WAS IN YOUR NEST?
THIS IS AN EGG! HOW COULD ANYONE NOT RECOGNIZE AN EGG?
THAT'S THE WORST EXCUSE I'VE EVER HEARD!
SIGH!
SCHULZ

MY DAD TOOK ME TO A BALL GAME YESTERDAY, CHARLIE BROWN..
THEY HAD A REAL DUGOUT, AND A WATER COOLER, AND A BAT RACK AND A DRESSING ROOM.. WE DON'T HAVE ANY OF THOSE THINGS!
DID YOU NOTICE SOMETHING ELSE THAT THEY HAD?
WHAT'S THAT?
REAL PLAYERS!
SCHULZ

YOU HAVE CUTE FINGERS, CHARLIE BROWN
HOW CAN ANYONE PITCH A BALL GAME WITH "CUTE FINGERS"?
SCHULZ

ALL RIGHT, GANG, LET'S KEEP AWAKE OUT THERE!
Z
Z
CLOMP!
ON THE OTHER HAND, FORGET I SAID ANYTHING!

AS LONG AS YOU'RE ALWAYS HAVING THESE DISCUSSIONS ON THE MOUND, CHARLIE BROWN, YOU SHOULD SERVE SOMETHING..
SERVE SOMETHING?
SURE, SOME KIND OF A LIGHT SNACK.. MILK AND COOKIES OR SOMETHING...
A NICE SALAD WOULD GO GOOD ON WARM DAYS...YES, A NICE FRUIT SALAD WITH MAYBE SOME ICED TEA...
SOME COLD MEAT WOULD PROBABLY BE NICE, TOO, AND..
AND IF I EVER MAKE THE MAJOR LEAGUES, I'LL PROBABLY PLAY ON AN EXPANSION CLUB...

IN CASE YOU DIDN'T KNOW, THE BALL DOESN'T HAVE TO STOP ROLLING BEFORE YOU CAN PICK IT UP!!
IT WAS HAVING A GOOD TIME, AND I DIDN'T WANT TO DISTURB IT
SCHULZ

AAUGH!!
HOW COULD YOU MISS SUCH AN EASY FLY BALL?
THE SUN GOT IN MY EYES
THE SUN ISN'T EVEN OUT TODAY! IT'S CLOUDY!
THE CLOUDS GOT IN MY EYES!
SCHULZ

LUCY, THAT'S THE FIFTH TIME TODAY YOU'VE STRUCK OUT!
YOU'RE SWINGING TOO HARD
ALL YOU HAVE TO DO IS MEET THE BALL
THAT'S WHAT I TRIED TO DO...
MY BAT WAS THERE, BUT THE BALL DIDN'T SHOW UP!
SCHULZ

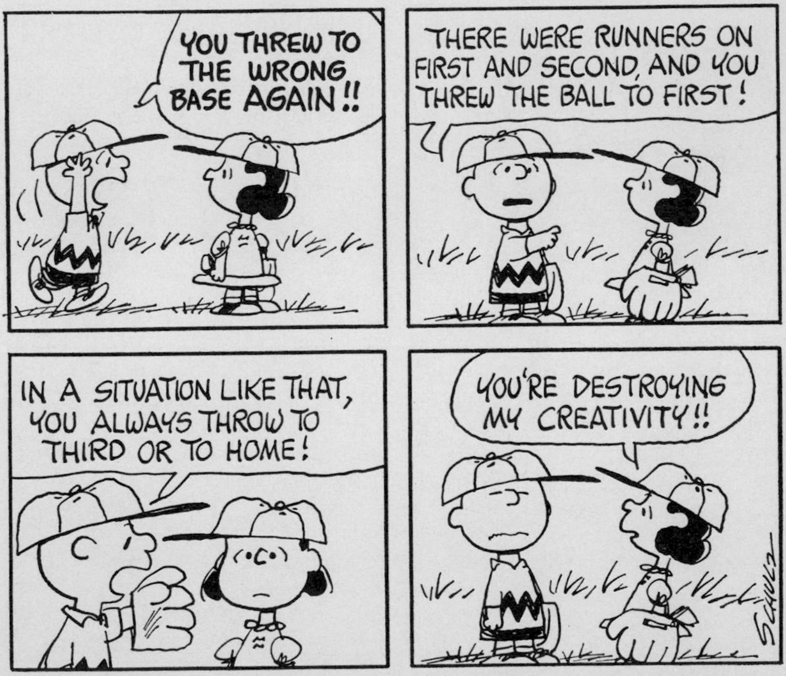
YOU THREW TO THE WRONG BASE AGAIN!!
THERE WERE RUNNERS ON FIRST AND SECOND, AND YOU THREW THE BALL TO FIRST!
IN A SITUATION LIKE THAT, YOU ALWAYS THROW TO THIRD OR TO HOME!
YOU'RE DESTROYING MY CREATIVITY!!
SCHULZ

DID YOU WANT TO SEE ME, MANAGER?
YES, LUCY...THIS IS VERY HARD FOR ME TO SAY, BUT I JUST DON'T THINK YOU'RE GOOD ENOUGH FOR OUR TEAM...
IF YOU KICK ME OFF THE TEAM, CHARLIE BROWN, I'LL NEVER SPEAK TO YOU AGAIN!
BUT I'LL SURE YELL AT YOU A LOT!!
SCHULZ

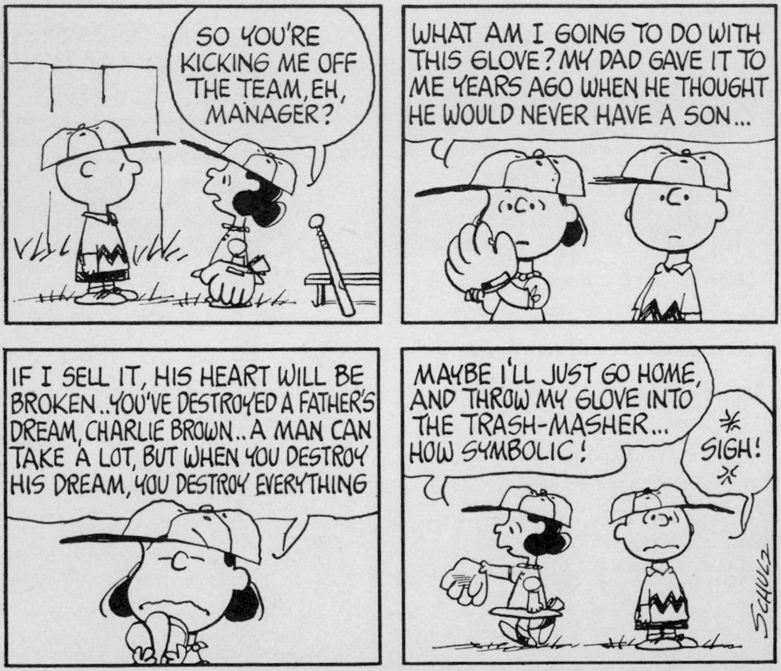
SO YOU'RE KICKING ME OFF THE TEAM, EH, MANAGER?
WHAT AM I GOING TO DO WITH THIS GLOVE? MY DAD GAVE IT TO ME YEARS AGO WHEN HE THOUGHT HE WOULD NEVER HAVE A SON...
IF I SELL IT, HIS HEART WILL BE BROKEN..YOU'VE DESTROYED A FATHER'S DREAM, CHARLIE BROWN..A MAN CAN TAKE A LOT, BUT WHEN YOU DESTROY HIS DREAM, YOU DESTROY EVERYTHING
MAYBE I'LL JUST GO HOME, AND THROW MY GLOVE INTO THE TRASH-MASHER... HOW SYMBOLIC!
SIGH!
SCHULZ

HOW COME YOU GET TO BE ON THE TEAM, AND I DON'T?
I'M A SUPERSTAR, SWEETIE!
SMAK
YOU STUPID BEAGLE!!!!
I THOUGHT SHE'D ENJOY BEING KISSED BY A SUPERSTAR...
SCHULZ

HEY, WHO TOLD YOU THAT YOU COULD PITCH?
YOU PITCH LIKE MY GRANDMOTHER! WHY DON'T YOU GIVE UP? YOU COULDN'T PITCH HAY! WHY DON'T YOU GO BACK WHERE YOU CAME FROM?! BOOOOOOO!!
IT'S HARD WORK BEING BITTER...
SCHULZ

IF WE CAN WIN THIS GAME TODAY, WE WON'T FINISH IN LAST PLACE
WELL, WITHOUT LUCY PLAYING, I THINK WE HAVE A CHANCE... I REALLY DO...
ISN'T IT NICE NOT HAVING HER AROUND? ISN'T IT NICE NOT HEARING HER VOICE?
ALL RIGHT, GET YOUR LUCKY-NUMBER SCORECARD RIGHT HERE!
SCHULZ

THIS IS IT... IF WE GET THIS LAST GUY, WE WIN... IF HE HITS ONE, WE LOSE...
IT'S A HIGH FLY BALL TO SNOOPY.... IF HE CATCHES IT, WE WIN!!
NO PROBLEM
HEY! WHO'S THE SHORTSTOP WITH THE BIG NOSE?
BIG NOSE?!!
BONK!
SCHULZ

AAUGH! WE LOST THE GAME!
WHAT HAPPENED?
SNOOPY GOT HIT ON THE HEAD WITH THE BALL!
WHY IS EVERYTHING SPINNING AROUND?
CALL THE VET, AND TELL HIM WE'RE BRINGING IN A PATIENT!!
CARRY ME GENTLY, MEN.. I'M A SUPERSTAR!
SCHULZ

I HATE LIFE! NO MATTER WHAT YOU DO, YOU ALWAYS END UP AT THE VET!
I'VE HEARD IT A MILLION TIMES, "TAKE HIM TO THE VET!"
"GIVE HIM A SHOT! GIVE HIM A PILL! HOLD HIM DOWN! PUT A MUZZLE ON HIM! LOCK HIM IN A KENNEL! CHAIN HIM TO A POST!"
NO WONDER DOGS. HOWL AT THE MOON!
SCHULZ

WHAT IN THE WORLD HAPPENED TO YOUR FINGER, CHARLIE BROWN?
WHEN SNOOPY GOT HIT ON THE HEAD BY THAT POP FLY, I TOOK HIM TO THE VET...THE VET SAID, "PUT YOUR DOG ON THE TABLE"
SNOOPY JUMPED OFF THE TABLE...I BENT DOWN TO PICK UP SNOOPY....
...THE VET STEPPED ON MY FINGER!
SCHULZ

THIS HAS BEEN A BAD TIME FOR ME..MAYBE IF I'M LUCKY, TOMORROW WILL BE A BETTER DAY
IN SOME PARTS OF THE WORLD, TOMORROW IS ALREADY TODAY AND TODAY IS YESTERDAY...
IF TOMORROW IS ALREADY TODAY, CHARLIE BROWN, THERE'S NO WAY THAT TOMORROW CAN BE A BETTER DAY
YOU'RE A LOT OF FUN TO HAVE AROUND
SCHULZ

I SAW A MOVIE RECENTLY ABOUT A BOY AND HIS DOG
THEY WERE STANDING BY A LAKE AS WE ARE, AND THE BOY PICKED UP A STICK AND THREW IT INTO THE WATER, AND THE DOG SWAM OUT AFTER IT AND BROUGHT IT BACK..
I'M GOING TO HAVE TO STOP WATCHING THOSE MOVIES
SCHULZ

SCHULZ

YO HO HO AND A BOTTLE OF RUM!
HERE'S THE FIERCE PIRATE STANDING ON THE DECK OF HIS SHIP...
HIS FAITHFUL PARROT FLIES TOWARD HIM TO PERCH ON HIS SHOULDER...
SCHULZ

WOODSTOCK HAS NEVER SEEN A VIOLIN OR A FIRE TRUCK OR A CANDY STORE..
HE'S NEVER HEARD AN OPERA OR A SYMPHONY...HE'S NEVER SEEN A MOVIE OR A PLAY...
ON THE OTHER HAND, HE'S SEEN THE SKY, THE CLOUDS, THE GROUND, THE SUN, THE RAIN, THE MOON, THE STARS, A CAT AND SEVERAL WORMS...
WOODSTOCK FEELS THAT HE'S LED A VERY FULL LIFE!
SCHULZ

RATS! I NEVER FIND ANY ARROWHEADS!
SCHULZ

DO YOU EVER FEEL LIKE RUNNING AWAY?
OF COURSE... SOMETIMES I FEEL LIKE I WANT TO RUN AWAY FROM EVERYTHING
I REMEMBER HAVING THAT FEELING ONCE WHEN I WAS AT THE DAISY HILL PUPPY FARM..
I CLIMBED OVER THE FENCE, BUT I WAS STILL IN THE WORLD!
SCHULZ

I'M TIRED... I ONLY HAD TEN HOURS SLEEP LAST NIGHT
TEN HOURS SHOULD BE PLENTY
NOT FOR ME... I HAVE BIG EYES..
IT'S A MEDICAL FACT THAT PEOPLE WITH BIG EYES NEED MORE SLEEP THAN PEOPLE WITH SMALL EYES...
PEOPLE WITH BIG STOMACHS NEED MORE FOOD, DON'T THEY?
SCHULZ

I TALKED WITH MY OPHTHALMOLOGIST TODAY
SO?
HE SAID THAT ALL HUMAN EYES ARE VERY CLOSE TO TWENTY-FIVE MILLIMETERS IN DIAMETER..HE SAID THAT SOME PEOPLE'S EYES APPEAR LARGER BECAUSE OF A WIDE LID FISSURE
THEREFORE, IT IS NOT TRUE THAT PEOPLE WITH LARGE EYES NEED MORE SLEEP THAN PEOPLE WITH SMALL EYES...
I KNOW A KID IN SCHOOL WHO BELONGS TO FOUR BOOK CLUBS!
SCHULZ

PSYCHIATRIC HELP 5¢
THE DOCTOR IS WAY OUT
PSYCHIATRIC HELP 5¢
I NEED SOME ADVICE
THE DOCTOR IS IN
GOOD..THAT'S WHAT I'M HERE FOR..
THE DOCTOR IS IN
THERE'S THIS BOY I KIND OF LIKE, SEE, BUT HE NEVER PAYS ANY ATTENTION TO ME.. IS IT BECAUSE I'M UNATTRACTIVE?
THE DOCTOR IS IN
HELP 5¢
NONSENSE! YOU'RE A VERY BEAUTIFUL YOUNG GIRL, AND YOU SHOULDN'T HAVE TO CHASE AFTER ANYONE!
THE DOCTOR
DO YOU REALLY THINK SO?
HE DOCTOR IS IN
OF COURSE! WOULD I LIE TO YOU?
THE DOCTOR IS IN
MY PSYCHIATRIST SAYS, "BLEAH!!
SCHULZ

I THINK IT WAS ONE OF THE BEST MOVIES I'VE EVER SEEN...
I KNEW YOU'D LIKE IT
SIP!
AFTERWARD, WE WENT TO THIS ART GALLERY, AND SAW ALL OF THESE WILD NEW PAINTINGS...
SOME OF THEM, OF COURSE, WERE QUITE HUGE...
THERE WAS ONE THAT WAS ALL DIFFERENT SHADES OF RED..
SIP!
I LIKE RED, OF COURSE, BUT I'M NOT SURE IF I LIKE IT THAT MUCH, AND..
SIP!
HI! DRINKING LEMONADE, I SEE! HOW ABOUT LETTING ME HAVE A SIP?
DON'T BE STUPID!!
SIP!
YOU THINK I WANT TO SIP FROM THE SAME STRAW YOU'VE BEEN SLURPING ON?! GET OUT OF HERE!
ANYWAY, THERE WERE A LOT OF NICE PAINTINGS, AND..
SIP!
YOU KNOW, IT'S HARD TO TALK TO YOU WHEN YOU KEEP MAKING ALL THOSE STRANGE FACES!
SCHULZ

YOU'RE LAZY, DO YOU KNOW THAT?
YOU'VE BEEN LAZY SINCE THE DAY YOU WERE BORN!
NOT "BORN".... "WHELPED"
SOME PEOPLE NEVER GET ANYTHING RIGHT
SCHULZ

I MISSED THE GOLDEN AGE OF VAUDEVILLE..
I MISSED THE GOLDEN AGE OF RADIO..
I MISSED THE GOLDEN AGE OF TELEVISION...
I REFUSE TO MISS THE GOLDEN AGE OF SLEEPING!
SCHULZ

Z,z (zeta)
A Tale of Two Cities
REALLY?
Of Human Bondage
YOU'RE KIDDING!
Heart of Darkness
I CAN'T BELIEVE IT!!
I HAVE A GREAT IDEA FOR A NOVEL, BUT ALL THE GOOD TITLES ARE TAKEN!
SCHULZ

"♡"
HERE'S THE WORLD-FAMOUS AUTHOR STARTING TO WORK ON HIS NEW NOVEL...
"I love you," she said. "I love you more than I can say."
"I love you, too," he answered.
"My love for you is higher than the highest mountain which is Mount Everest which is over twenty-nine thousand feet high."
"My love for you is deeper than the deepest ocean which is the Marianas trench which is over thirty-five thousand feet deep."
MY HERO IS A TERRIBLE BORE!
SCHULZ

THAT WAS A GOOD DIVE..
HAD IT BEEN INTO MY WATER DISH, I WOULD EVEN CALL IT A BEAUTIFUL DIVE...HOWEVER, IT WAS NOT INTO MY WATER DISH... IT WAS INTO MY SUPPER DISH!
SCHULZ

MY BEACH BALL JUST FLOATED AWAY
IT PROBABLY FLOATED CLEAR ACROSS TO THE OTHER SIDE OF THE WORLD WHERE ANOTHER LITTLE KID FOUND IT, AND IS PLAYING WITH IT...
LUCKY KID!!
SCHULZ

YOU STUPID KID, WHO LIVES CLEAR ACROSS ON THE OTHER SIDE OF THE WORLD, SEND BACK MY BEACH BALL!!
WHAT ARE YOU, A COMMUNIST OR SOMETHING?!
SCHULZ

MY BEACH BALL! IT'S COMING BACK!
THAT KID ON THE OTHER SIDE OF THE WORLD SENT IT BACK! OUR NATIONS ARE IN HARMONY!
THE WIND CHANGED
TWO NATIONS, USING TWO INNOCENT CHILDREN AND A BEACH BALL, HAVE DEMONSTRATED TO THE WORLD THAT THEY CAN LIVE IN TOTAL HARMONY!
THE WIND CHANGED
SCHULZ

DEAR SIR...
D x y 2 R k i Q L & ! c " h m s --- ? 3 d ? f B *
MY SECRETARY ISN'T USED TO AN ELECTRIC TYPEWRITER!
SCHULZ

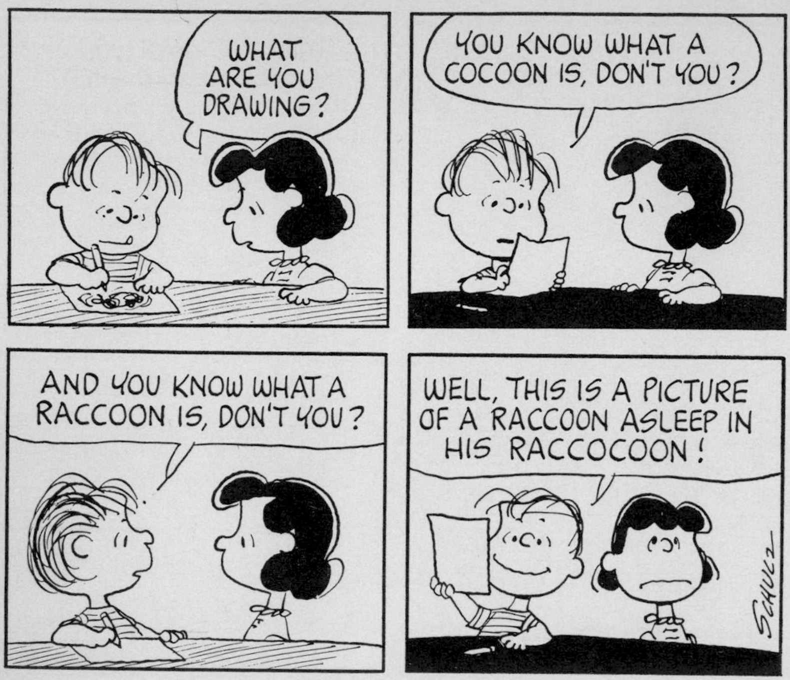
WHAT ARE YOU DRAWING?
YOU KNOW WHAT A COCOON IS, DON'T YOU?
AND YOU KNOW WHAT A RACCOON IS, DON'T YOU?
WELL, THIS IS A PICTURE OF A RACCOON ASLEEP IN HIS RACCOCOON!
SCHULZ

YOU'RE PROBABLY THE MOST WISHY-WASHY PERSON I'VE EVER KNOWN!
YOU'RE REALLY NOT MUCH USE TO ANYONE, CHARLIE BROWN! YOU'RE WEAK, AND DUMB, AND BORING, AND HOPELESS!!
INCIDENTALLY, HOW COME I NEVER HEAR YOU SING ANYMORE?
SCHULZ

WELL, OL' MOUND, THE BASEBALL SEASON IS OVER FOR US...
WE MAY NOT HAVE WON ANY GAMES, BUT WE HAD GREAT TIMES, DIDN'T WE? SO LONG... I'LL SEE YOU AGAIN NEXT YEAR..
SIGH
SCHULZ

SCHOOL STARTS AGAIN NEXT WEEK...
I THINK I'VE RUINED HER EYES FOR GOOD!
SCHULZ

LATELY EVERYTHING SEEMS TO BOTHER ME...
HOW DO YOU MEAN?
WHAT DO YOU THINK SECURITY IS, CHUCK?
SECURITY?
SECURITY IS SLEEPING IN THE BACK SEAT OF THE CAR...
WHEN YOU'RE A LITTLE KID, AND YOU'VE BEEN SOMEWHERE WITH YOUR MOM AND DAD, AND IT'S NIGHT, AND YOU'RE RIDING HOME IN THE CAR, YOU CAN SLEEP IN THE BACK SEAT..
YOU DON'T HAVE TO WORRY ABOUT ANYTHING... YOUR MOM AND DAD ARE IN THE FRONT SEAT, AND THEY DO ALL THE WORRYING...THEY TAKE CARE OF EVERYTHING...
THAT'S REAL NEAT!
BUT IT DOESN'T LAST! SUDDENLY, YOU'RE GROWN UP, AND IT CAN NEVER BE THAT WAY AGAIN!
SUDDENLY, IT'S OVER, AND YOU'LL NEVER GET TO SLEEP IN THE BACK SEAT AGAIN! NEVER!
NEVER?
ABSOLUTELY NEVER!
HOLD MY HAND, CHUCK!!
SCHULZ

FINISH
THE YEARS ARE GOING BY..
I'M SCARED, CHUCK... WHAT IF I GROW UP, AND NO ONE EVER LOVES ME? WE PEOPLE WITH BIG NOSES ARE VERY INSECURE...
DO YOU THINK I HAVE A BIG NOSE, CHUCK? DO YOU THINK SOMEONE WILL LOVE ME SOMEDAY?
SURE
SURE?! "SURE," WHAT? "SURE" I HAVE A BIG NOSE, OR "SURE" SOMEONE WILL LOVE ME SOMEDAY?
MAYBE SOMEDAY THE REST OF YOUR FACE WILL CATCH UP WITH YOUR NOSE, AND THEN SOMEONE WILL LOVE YOU
HURRY UP, FACE!
SCHULZ

WARRANTY
HERE YOU GO, OL' PAL..
ENJOY YOUR SUPPER
!
HOLD IT!
I THINK I LEFT SOMETHING OUT...
I'M THE ONLY ONE I KNOW WHO HAS EVER HAD HIS SUPPER RECALLED!
SCHULZ

boot
boot boot boot boot
boot boot boot boot boot
boot boot
I'M GLAD I CAN'T HEAR WHAT HOWARD COSELL IS SAYING ABOUT THIS...
SCHULZ

KLUNK!
THAT'S WHAT IS CALLED "COMING IN OFF THE BENCH"
SCHULZ

STOMP!
RAH?
SCHULZ

SCHULZ

BONK!
WOODSTOCK HAS DIFFICULTY RECOVERING FUMBLES...
SCHULZ

THAT STUPID WOODSTOCK... HE LOST HIS BOOK WITH ALL OUR SECRET PLAYS!
TWENTY THOUSAND LAPS AROUND THE FIELD!
SCHULZ

WHAT A LOUSY BREAK!
NO WONDER COACHES GO CRAZY...
FIRST GAME OF THE SEASON, AND WHAT HAPPENS?
MY MIDDLE LINEBACKER GETS HIS HEAD CAUGHT IN HIS LOCKER!
SCHULZ

PUNT!
BONK!!
IF YOU DON'T PLAY EVERY DAY, YOU LOSE THAT FINE EDGE...
SCHULZ

boot!
!
SCHULZ

SMAK!
POMPON GIRLS CAN'T RESIST A SUPERSTAR!
SCHULZ

MY DAD SAYS THAT LIFE IS LIKE A GAME OF GOLF
DO YOU THINK HE'S RIGHT ?
ABSOLUTELY
AND I FEEL LIKE I'VE JUST BOGEYED THE LAST FIVE HOLES !
SCHULZ

I HAVE A SURPRISE FOR YOU...
THIS IS A NEW DOG FOOD WITH Q-800 ADDED PLUS R-455, M-17 AND W-9000
JUST WHAT I NEEDED... A BOWL FULL OF NUMBERS !
SCHULZ

"PROBLEM NUMBER FIVE.."
"A MAN HAS A DAUGHTER AND A SON..THE SON IS THREE YEARS OLDER THAN THE DAUGHTER.."
"IN ONE YEAR THE MAN WILL BE SIX TIMES AS OLD AS THE DAUGHTER IS NOW, AND IN TEN YEARS HE WILL BE FOURTEEN YEARS OLDER THAN THE COMBINED AGES OF HIS CHILDREN... WHAT IS THE MAN'S PRESENT AGE?"
I'M SORRY, WE ARE UNABLE TO COMPLETE YOUR CALL..PLEASE CHECK THE NUMBER AND DIAL AGAIN!
SCHULZ

LEAF CROSSING
SCHULZ

DO YOU WANT TO HEAR SOMETHING ROMANTIC?
IF YOU GAVE ME A ROSE, I'D TAKE ONE OF THE PETALS AND PRESS IT BETWEEN THE PAGES OF A BOOK...
WOULDN'T THAT BE ROMANTIC?
YOU CAN'T PRESS A ROSE PETAL IN A COMIC BOOK!
SCHULZ

I THINK EVERY WEEK SHOULD HAVE ONE DAY IN IT WHEN BOYS GIVE PRESENTS TO GIRLS
I THINK I'LL SUGGEST THAT
WHO ARE YOU GOING TO SUGGEST IT TO?
I DON'T KNOW...
BUT I'LL SUGGEST IT!
SCHULZ

YOU HAVE NO IDEA HOW IMPORTANT IT IS FOR A GIRL TO GET PRESENTS
IF NO ONE GIVES HER PRESENTS, HER LIFE HAS NO MEANING!
AREN'T YOU INTERESTED IN THE MEANING OF LIFE?
SCHULZ

YOU KNOW WHAT BEETHOVEN NEVER HAD?
BEETHOVEN NEVER HAD GIRLS HANGING ON HIS PIANO BUGGING HIM ABOUT SENDING THEM PRESENTS!
HE DIDN'T?
POOR BEETHOVEN!
SCHULZ

IF A BOY NEVER SENDS A GIRL FLOWERS, HE ROBS HIMSELF OF ONE OF THE GREAT JOYS OF LIFE...
THIEF! ROBBER!!
SCHULZ

To Whom It May Concern;
Dear Whom,
SCHULZ

PROBABLY A SCARECROW
?
THIS IS KIND OF INTERESTING... WOODSTOCK SAYS HE SORT OF FIGURED IT WAS A SCARECROW..
HE SAYS THAT HE KNEW ALL ALONG IT WASN'T A REAL HUMAN BEING BECAUSE MOST HUMAN BEINGS ARE NOT THAT FOND OF STANDING FOR SUCH A LENGTH OF TIME IN THE HOT SUN...
HE SAYS THE FACT THAT THE CLOTHES ARE OUT OF STYLE ALSO MADE HIM A LITTLE SUSPICIOUS..
BLEAH!
WOODSTOCK WOULD HAVE MADE A GOOD CROW!
SCHULZ

GO STRAIGHT OUT, SNOOPY, AND THEN CUT LEFT... I'LL FAKE A RUN, AND PASS IT...
DO YOU THINK THAT'S A GOOD PLAY?
SMAK!
HE THINKS IT'S A GOOD PLAY!
SCHULZ

ALL RIGHT, TEAM, LET'S PAY ATTENTION
WE'RE HERE TODAY TO TRY TO EVALUATE OUR PERFORMANCES ON THE FIELD...EACH OF US CAN STAND A LITTLE IMPROVEMENT...
EACH OF US CAN LEARN SOMETHING IF WE'RE WILLING TO ACCEPT CRITICISM...
YOUR NOSE IS TOO BIG!
SCHULZ

WELL, HERE I AM AGAIN FOR "SHOW AND TELL"
AND GUESS WHAT I'VE BROUGHT TODAY! I HAVE THINGS IN HERE TO THRILL YOU AND CHILL YOU! I HAVE THINGS IN HERE TO FILL YOU WITH FEAR, WITH TERROR, WITH HORROR! I HAVE THINGS IN HERE TO...
...YES, MA'AM?
ALL THE LIFE HAS GONE OUT OF "SHOW AND TELL"
SCHULZ

Science Report; "Forest Strangers"
Our wild life and our trees are protected by brave and dedicated men.
These men live by themselves in towers and are called Forest Strangers.
I WONDER IF I SHOULD INCLUDE AN EXPLANATION OF HOW THEY GOT THAT NAME..
PROBABLY NOT
SCHULZ

!
A WORM TWO FEET LONG? THAT'S RIDICULOUS!
SCHULZ

WOODSTOCK GIVES BORING PARTIES!
SCHULZ

COLUMNIST
HERE'S ONE FROM IOWA...AND HERE'S ONE FROM PENNSYLVANIA..
Advice For Dog Owners
type type type
"DEAR SIR, I HAVE A DOG WHO CONTINUALLY SCRATCHES HIS EARS...WHAT SHOULD I DO? SIGNED, 'WONDERING'"
Dear Wondering, What I'm wondering is how you can be so dumb! Take your dog to the vet right away, stupid.
type type type type
"DEAR SIR, WE HAVE THREE PUPPIES WHO HAVE ENLARGED JOINTS AND ARE LAME... WHAT DO YOU THINK CAUSED THIS, AND WHAT SHOULD WE DO? SIGNED, 'DOG OWNER'"
Dear Dog Owner, Why don't you take up rock collecting? You're too stupid to be a dog owner. In the meantime, call your vet immediately.
type type type type
"DEAR SIR, MY DOG HAS BEEN COUGHING LATELY... WHAT SHOULD I DO? SIGNED, 'CONFUSED'"
Dear Confused, You're not confused, you're just not very smart. Now, you get that dog to the vet right away before I come over and punch you in the nose!
type type type
I WRITE A VERY FIRM COLUMN!
SCHULZ

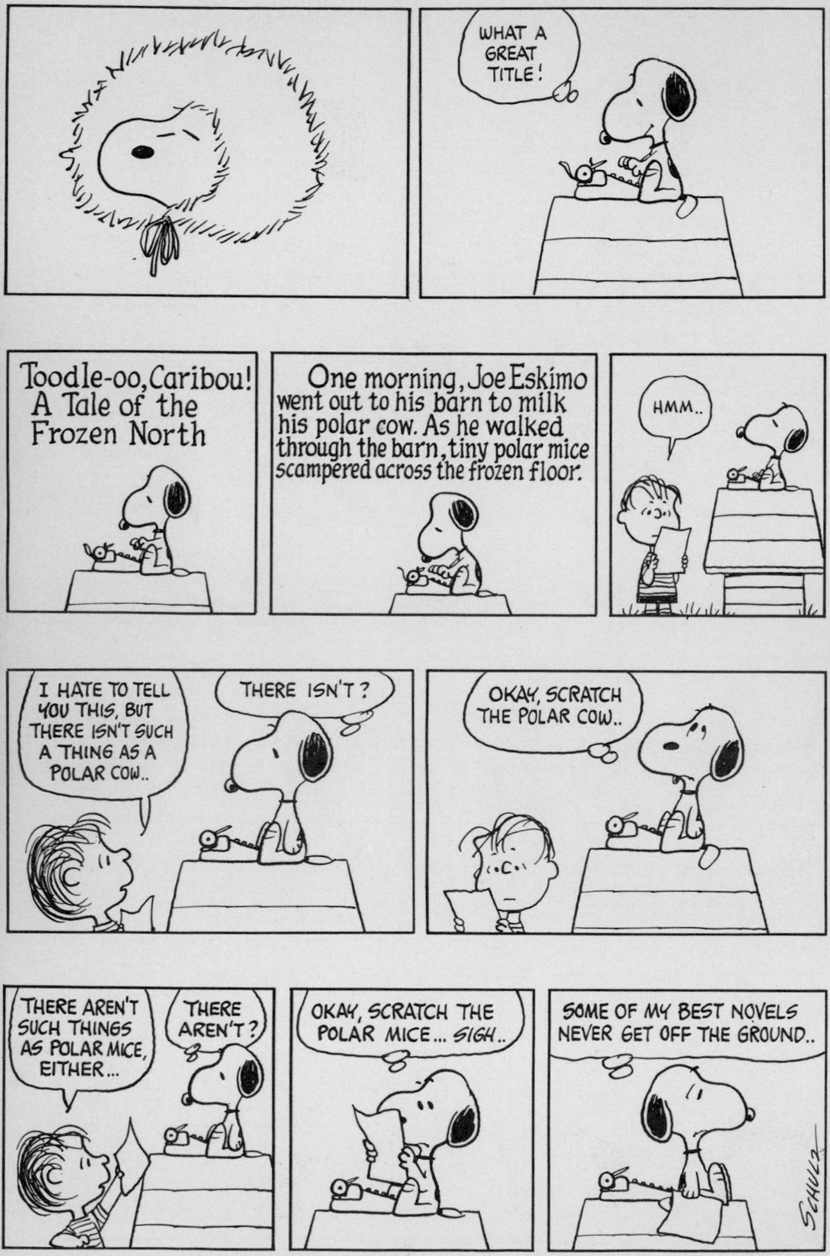
WHAT A GREAT TITLE!
Toodle-oo, Caribou! A Tale of the Frozen North
One morning, Joe Eskimo went out to his barn to milk his polar cow. As he walked through the barn, tiny polar mice scampered across the frozen floor.
HMM..
I HATE TO TELL YOU THIS, BUT THERE ISN'T SUCH A THING AS A POLAR COW..
THERE ISN'T?
OKAY, SCRATCH THE POLAR COW..
THERE AREN'T SUCH THINGS AS POLAR MICE, EITHER...
THERE AREN'T?
OKAY, SCRATCH THE POLAR MICE... SIGH..
SOME OF MY BEST NOVELS NEVER GET OFF THE GROUND..
SCHULZ

type
type
type
type
Toodle-oo, Caribou! A Tale of the Frozen North
The stall was empty! "Someone has stolen my polar cow!" shouted Joe Eskimo.
"This is the work of Joe Jacket, who hates me!"
MAY I SEE HOW YOUR NEW NOVEL IS COMING ALONG?
BE MY GUEST..
"JOE ESKIMO AND JOE JACKET WERE RIVALS FOR THE HEART OF SALLY SNOW WHO LIVED SOUTH OF THE ICEBERG...JOE ESKIMO THOUGHT BACK TO THE NIGHT HE FIRST SHOOK HER HAND"
"'I THINK YOU ARE VERY NICE,' HE HAD TOLD HER, AND THEY SHOOK HANDS."
THEY SHOOK HANDS?
I THINK YOUR LOVE SCENE NEEDS A LITTLE SOMETHING..
I ALWAYS GET SO EMBARRASSED..
SCHULZ

I SIGNED UP FOR A NEW COURSE TODAY
IT'S CALLED "INTRODUCTION TO MATH"
IS IT HARD?
NOT AT ALL..
I JUST WALKED RIGHT IN, AND SAID, "HOW DO YOU DO, MATH!"
SCHULZ

MY FAVORITE HOCKEY TEAM DIDN'T DO TOO WELL LAST YEAR...
THIS SEASON, HOWEVER, THEY HAVE HIGH HOPES..
DID THEY GET SOME NEW PLAYERS?
NO, THEY BOUGHT A NEW PUCK!
SCHULZ

HERE... A MESSAGE JUST CAME FOR YOU..
A MESSAGE?
IT MUST BE FROM THE "HEAD BEAGLE"... IT'S IN CODE!
SCHULZ

YOU GOT A CODED MESSAGE FROM THE HEAD BEAGLE?
CAN YOU READ IT? HAVE YOU FIGURED IT OUT? WHAT DOES IT SAY?
I CAN'T BELIEVE IT...
"THOMPSON IS IN TROUBLE!"
THOMPSON?! WHO IS THOMPSON?
THAT STUPID THOMPSON! HE'S DONE IT AGAIN!!
SCHULZ

WHAT IN THE WORLD IS THIS?
SNOOPY GOT A MESSAGE FROM THE HEAD BEAGLE... IT'S IN CODE...
WHAT DOES IT SAY?
IT SAYS, "THOMPSON IS IN TROUBLE!"
FOR A JOB LIKE THIS, I HAVE TO PUT ON MY FAMOUS DISGUISE...
THAT STUPID THOMPSON! THE LAST TIME THIS HAPPENED, HE ALMOST GOT US ALL KILLED...
SCHULZ

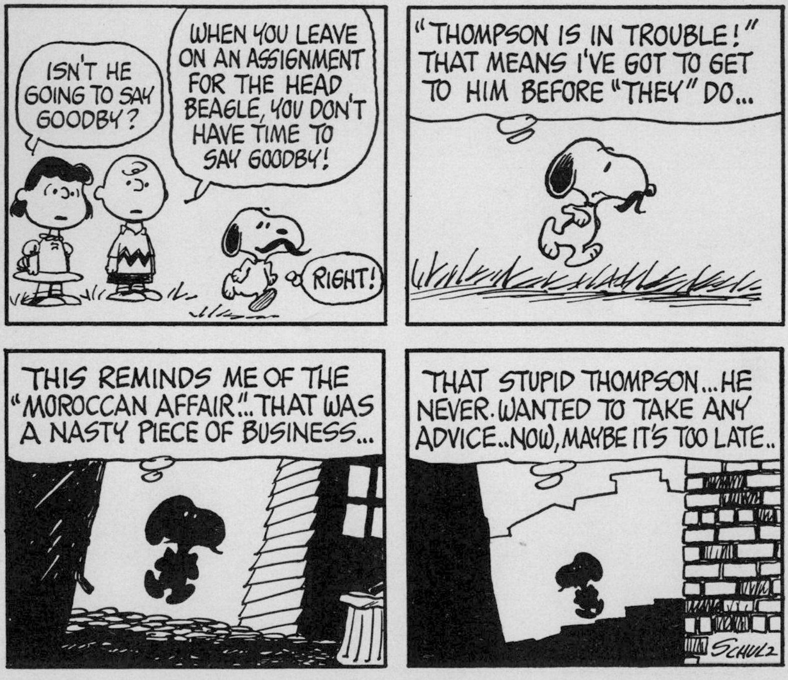
ISN'T HE GOING TO SAY GOODBY?
WHEN YOU LEAVE ON AN ASSIGNMENT FOR THE HEAD BEAGLE, YOU DON'T HAVE TIME TO SAY GOODBY!
RIGHT!
"THOMPSON IS IN TROUBLE!" THAT MEANS I'VE GOT TO GET TO HIM BEFORE "THEY" DO...
THIS REMINDS ME OF THE "MOROCCAN AFFAIR"!.. THAT WAS A NASTY PIECE OF BUSINESS...
THAT STUPID THOMPSON...HE NEVER WANTED TO TAKE ANY ADVICE..NOW, MAYBE IT'S TOO LATE..
SCHULZ

THOMPSON ?
THOMPSON ?
HMM...THERE'S A LITTLE RESTAURANT THAT LOOKS FULL OF SHADY TYPES...
MAYBE THE WAITRESS KNOWS THOMPSON... I'LL GO IN, AND SLYLY STRIKE UP A CONVERSATION WITH HER...
HI, SWEETIE!
SCHULZ

UH...IT'S LIKE THIS, SWEETIE...
I'M KIND OF LOOKING FOR A CHARACTER NAMED THOMPSON, SEE, AND I SORTA NEED YOUR HELP
HE'S ABOUT FOURTEEN INCHES... CARRIES A GOOD STRAIGHT LINE, HARKS TO THE TRACK, HAS A QUICK CLAIMING MOUTH RIGHT IN THE GROUND AND HAS A GOOD PEDIGREE
SHE KNOWS HIM !!
SCHULZ

THAT WAITRESS SAID SHE SAW THOMPSON HEADING NORTH OF TOWN..
THAT STUPID THOMPSON! THIS IS JUST THE SORT OF THING I KNEW HE'D DO!
I SHOULD BE BACK IN THE RESTAURANT QUAFFING ROOT BEERS WITH THAT WAITRESS... I THINK SHE KIND OF LIKED ME..
NOW, IT'S RAINING, AND I'M GETTING ALL WET AND I'M PROBABLY LOST... THAT STUPID THOMPSON!!
SCHULZ

THOMPSON?
THOMPSON, WHERE ARE YOU?
THOMPSON?
!
TOO LATE!
POOR THOMPSON!
SCHULZ

Report to the Head Beagle
Subject: Our Beagle in the field, Thompson.
Subject attempted to subdue ten thousand rabbits by himself. End came quickly.
Rabbit-tat-tat, and it was all over!
SCHULZ

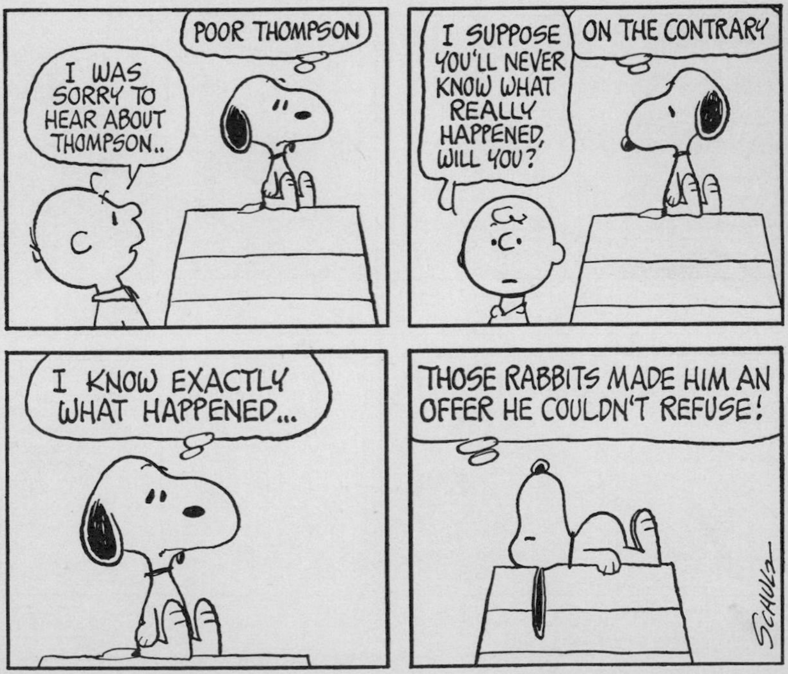
I WAS SORRY TO HEAR ABOUT THOMPSON..
POOR THOMPSON
I SUPPOSE YOU'LL NEVER KNOW WHAT REALLY HAPPENED, WILL YOU?
ON THE CONTRARY
I KNOW EXACTLY WHAT HAPPENED...
THOSE RABBITS MADE HIM AN OFFER HE COULDN'T REFUSE!
SCHULZ

CHARLIE BROWNNNN
I'LL HOLD THE FOOTBALL, CHARLIE BROWN, AND YOU COME RUNNING UP, AND KICK IT..
I CAN'T
I NEVER DO ANYTHING WITHOUT CONSULTING MY PSYCHIATRIST...
WELL, YOU GO TALK WITH YOUR PSYCHIATRIST, AND SEE WHAT YOU WANT TO DO... OKAY?
PSYCHIATRIC HELP 5¢
THE DOCTOR IS IN
I HAVE A STRANGE PROBLEM
THERE'S THIS GIRL, SEE, AND SHE'S ALWAYS TRYING TO GET ME TO KICK THIS FOOTBALL, BUT SHE ALSO ALWAYS PULLS IT AWAY AND I LAND ON MY BACK AND KILL MYSELF...
SHE SOUNDS LIKE AN INTERESTING GIRL... SORT OF A FUN TYPE...
I GET THE IMPRESSION THAT YOU HAVE A REAL NEED TO KICK THIS FOOTBALL... I THINK YOU SHOULD TRY IT!
I THINK YOU SHOULD TRY IT BECAUSE IN MEDICAL TERMS, YOU HAVE WHAT WE CALL THE "NEED TO NEED TO TRY IT"
I'M GLAD I TALKED WITH MY PSYCHIATRIST BECAUSE THIS YEAR I'M GONNA KICK THAT BALL CLEAR TO THE MOON!
AUGH!
WHAM
UNFORTUNATELY, CHARLIE BROWN, YOUR AVERAGE PSYCHIATRIST KNOWS VERY LITTLE ABOUT KICKING FOOTBALLS
SCHULZ

Z
SCHULZ

WELL, AT LEAST THEY CAN RUN FASTER...
HOW CAN YOU TALK TO SOMEONE WHO KEEPS SAYING, "AU CONTRAIRE"?
SCHULZ

I GOT SIX COMPLIMENTS TODAY...
FANTASTIC!
IT'S NOT OFTEN YOU CAN GET SIX COMPLIMENTS IN ONE DAY
TWO OF THEM WERE EVEN SINCERE!
SCHULZ

I WORRIED ABOUT THIS TEST ALL NIGHT..
I WORRIED AND WORRIED AND WORRIED...
SO WHAT HAPPENED?
I GOT AN "A"
I WASTED A GOOD WORRY!
SCHULZ

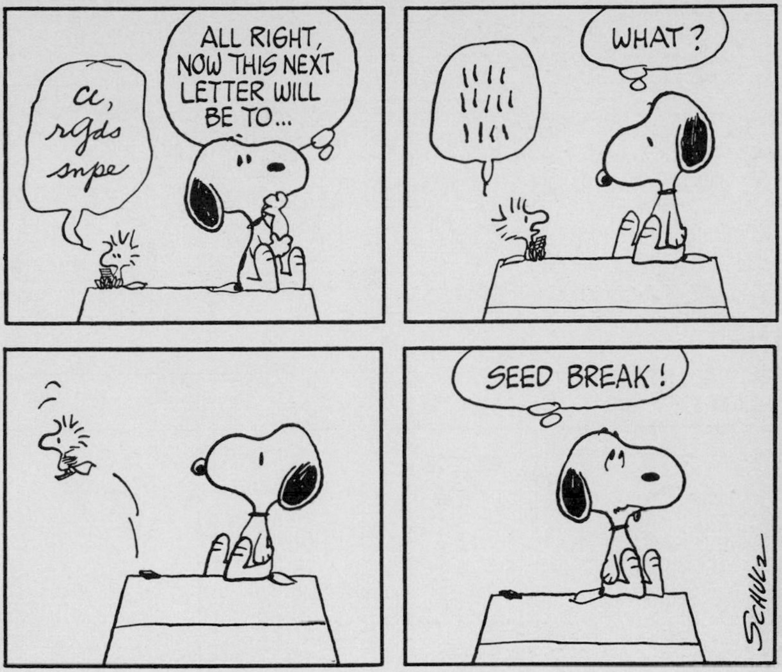
a, rgds snpe
ALL RIGHT, NOW THIS NEXT LETTER WILL BE TO...
WHAT?
SEED BREAK!
SCHULZ

DEAR SIR...
ds
IS THERE REALLY SUCH A THING AS A "WORM BREAK"?
SCHULZ

!
!
?
"FEAR OF FALLING LEAVES."... WHEN WE GET HOME, I'LL HAVE TO LOOK THAT ONE UP...
SCHULZ

HMM..
IT SAYS HERE THAT THE HUMMINGBIRD IS THE ONLY WINGED CREATURE THAT CAN FLAP HIS WINGS FAST ENOUGH TO BE ABLE TO HOVER MOTIONLESS IN THE AIR...
THAT'S VERY INTERESTING
KLUNK!
ONE-TENTH OF A SECOND IS NOT A HOVER!
SCHULZ

YES, MA'AM...WE'D LIKE TO BORROW THE LATEST BOOK BY MISS HELEN SWEETSTORY..
BANNED?!!
IT'S BEEN BANNED FROM THE SCHOOL LIBRARY! I CAN'T BELIEVE IT!
HOW COULD ANYONE BAN SUCH A NEAT BOOK AS "THE SIX BUNNY-WUNNIES FREAK OUT"?
SCHULZ

WHY WOULD THEY BAN MISS SWEETSTORY'S BOOK FROM THE SCHOOL LIBRARY?
I CAN'T BELIEVE IT.. I JUST CAN'T BELIEVE IT!
MAYBE THERE ARE SOME THINGS IN HER BOOK THAT WE DON'T UNDERSTAND...
IN THAT CASE, THEY SHOULD ALSO BAN MY MATH BOOK!
SCHULZ

YES, MA'AM, WE'D LIKE TO SEE THE PRINCIPAL IF HE'S NOT TOO BUSY...
WELL, IT'S KIND OF A PERSONAL MATTER...YES, MA'AM...WE'RE STUDENTS HERE..
WHAT DID YOU THINK WE WERE, ENCYCLOPEDIA SALESMEN?
WHATEVER HAPPENED TO GOOD OLD-FASHIONED TACT ?!
PRINCIPAL'S OFFICE
SCHULZ

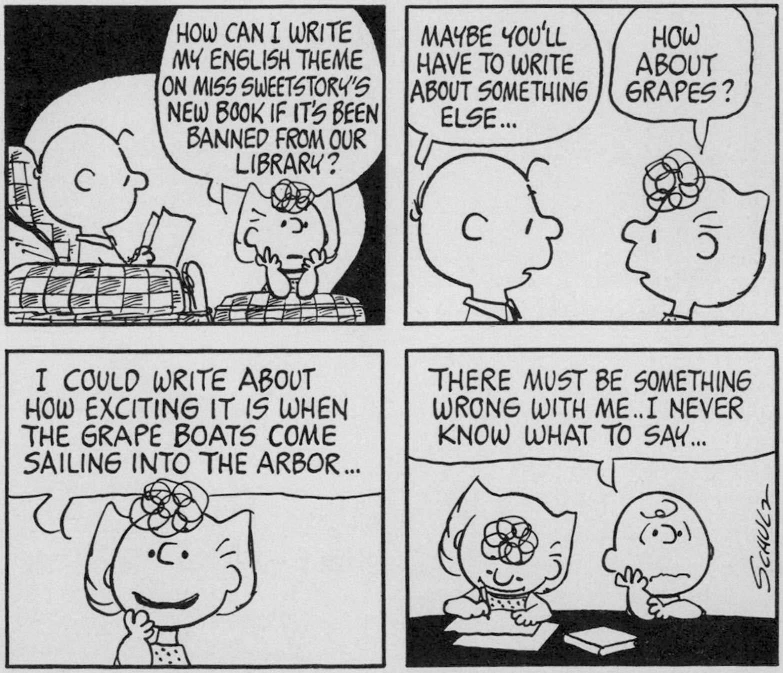
HOW CAN I WRITE MY ENGLISH THEME ON MISS SWEETSTORY'S NEW BOOK IF IT'S BEEN BANNED FROM OUR LIBRARY?
MAYBE YOU'LL HAVE TO WRITE ABOUT SOMETHING ELSE...
HOW ABOUT GRAPES?
I COULD WRITE ABOUT HOW EXCITING IT IS WHEN THE GRAPE BOATS COME SAILING INTO THE ARBOR...
THERE MUST BE SOMETHING WRONG WITH ME..I NEVER KNOW WHAT TO SAY...
SCHULZ

SCHOOL CROSSING
I'M MAD, CHARLIE BROWN!
THEY'VE BANNED HELEN SWEETSTORY'S BOOK FROM OUR SCHOOL LIBRARY, AND I CAN'T FIND OUT WHY!!
I'M SO MAD I FEEL LIKE SUING THE SCHOOL BOARD! I THINK I WOULD, TOO, IF I HAD AN ATTORNEY...
BEFORE I TAKE ANY CASE, I HAVE TO KNOW WHERE TO SEND THE BILL!
SCHULZ

ALL RIGHT, ATTORNEY, I'LL EXPLAIN OUR PROBLEM, AND YOU TELL ME IF WE HAVE A CASE..
"IMPOSSIBILITY IS AN EXCUSE IN LAW"
OUR SCHOOL LIBRARY HAS BANNED A CERTAIN BOOK, SEE, AND WE WANT TO FIND OUT WHY...
"ARREST THE DEBTOR TO SATISFY A JUDGMENT"
NOW, IT'S NOT SO MUCH A MATTER OF THE BOOK ITSELF AS WHY WE...
Z
SIGH
SCHULZ

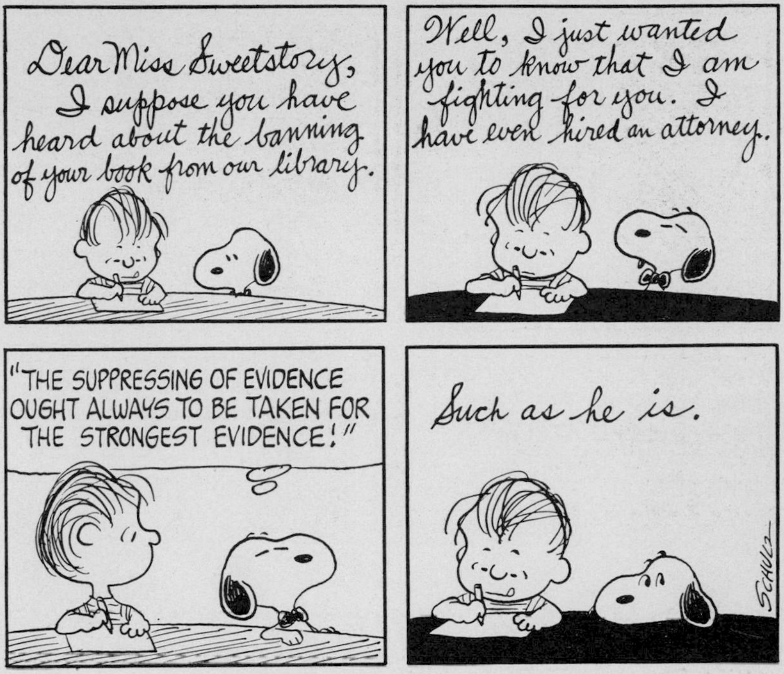
Dear Miss Sweetstory,
I suppose you have heard about the banning of your book from our library.
Well, I just wanted you to know that I am fighting for you. I have even hired an attorney.
"THE SUPPRESSING OF EVIDENCE OUGHT ALWAYS TO BE TAKEN FOR THE STRONGEST EVIDENCE!"
Such as he is.
SCHULZ

OKAY, ATTORNEY, LET'S MAKE A FEW PHONE CALLS, AND SEE WHAT WE CAN FIND OUT..
"WE KNOW THAT THE LAW IS GOOD IF A MAN USE IT LAWFULLY"
HELLO, SCHOOL BOARD?
I WONDER IF JOHN DOE OR RICHARD ROE WILL BE IN COURT... I HATE CASES THAT DON'T HAVE JOHN DOE OR RICHARD ROE..
YES, I'D LIKE TO SPEAK TO THE HEAD OF THE SCHOOL BOARD, PLEASE..
"THE CLIENT CARES LITTLE FOR A 'BEAUTIFUL' CASE"
SCHULZ

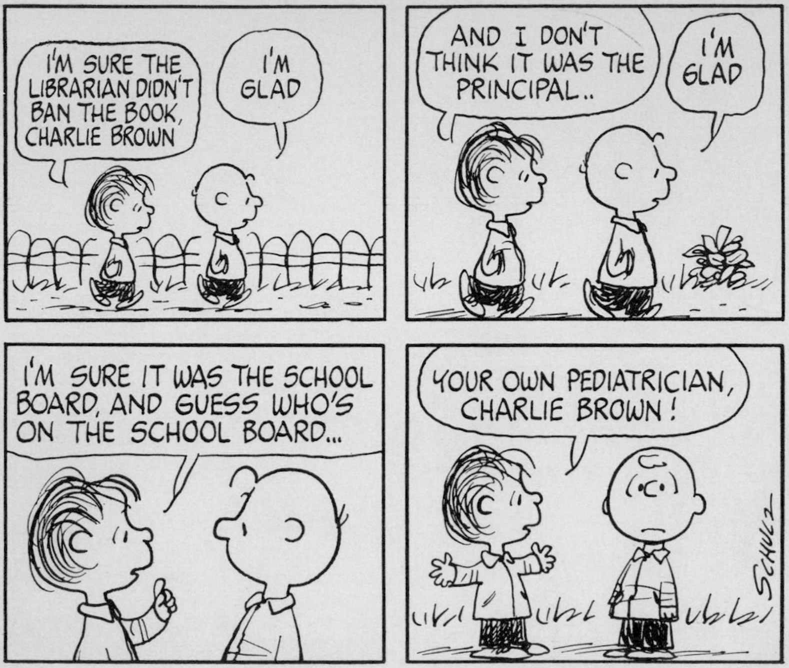
I'M SURE THE LIBRARIAN DIDN'T BAN THE BOOK, CHARLIE BROWN
I'M GLAD
AND I DON'T THINK IT WAS THE PRINCIPAL..
I'M GLAD
I'M SURE IT WAS THE SCHOOL BOARD, AND GUESS WHO'S ON THE SCHOOL BOARD...
YOUR OWN PEDIATRICIAN, CHARLIE BROWN!
SCHULZ

YOU WANT **ME** TO TALK TO MY OWN DOCTOR ABOUT MISS SWEETSTORY'S BOOK?
WHY NOT? HE'S ON THE SCHOOL BOARD, ISN'T HE? HE WAS THE ONE WHO BANNED HER BOOK!
DO PEOPLE REALLY TALK TO DOCTORS?
OF COURSE, CHARLIE BROWN.. EVERY DAY...
DO THE DOCTORS LISTEN?
SCHULZ

YES, MA'AM, I'D LIKE TO TALK TO THE DOCTOR...
NO, I FEEL FINE... I'D JUST LIKE TO TALK TO HIM FOR A MINUTE...
I SEE...
IF I GO BACK OUTSIDE, AND CATCH A COLD, THEN MAY I TALK TO HIM?
SCHULZ

GOOD AFTERNOON, DOCTOR..
I'M FINE, THANK YOU... YES, I THINK I'VE BEEN FEELING VERY WELL LATELY...
I APPRECIATE YOUR SEEING ME LIKE THIS...
I WAS AFRAID YOU MIGHT THINK IT WAS A WASTE OF TIME TALKING TO A WELL PERSON..
SCHULZ

YOU'RE MY DOCTOR, SIR, AND I RESPECT YOU...
HOWEVER, I'VE COME TO SEE YOU BECAUSE I HAVE TO KNOW WHY YOU AND THE SCHOOL BOARD BANNED "THE SIX BUNNY WUNNIES FREAK OUT" FROM OUR LIBRARY...
KLUNK!!
!
SOMEHOW, YOU NEVER EXPECT A DOCTOR TO FAINT...
SCHULZ

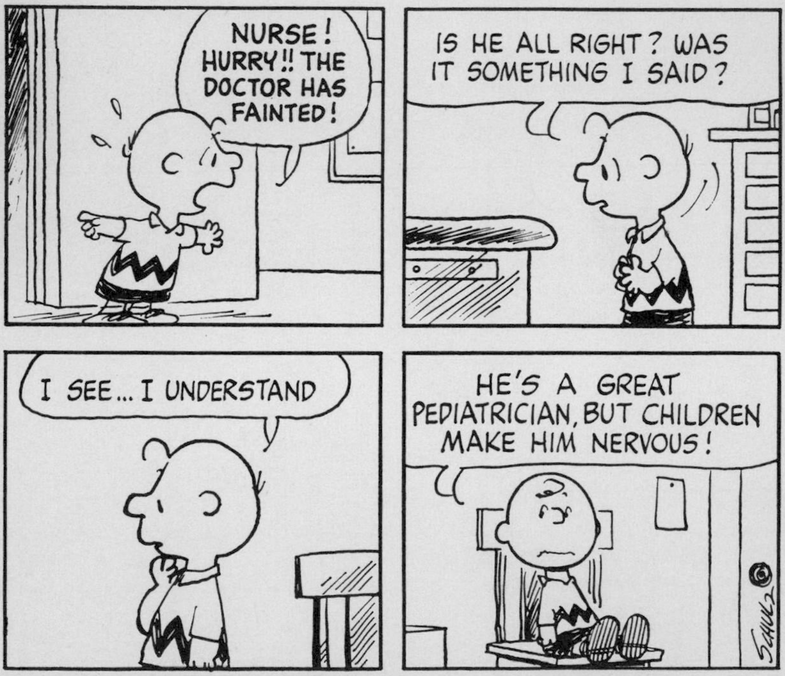
NURSE! HURRY!! THE DOCTOR HAS FAINTED!
IS HE ALL RIGHT? WAS IT SOMETHING I SAID?
I SEE... I UNDERSTAND
HE'S A GREAT PEDIATRICIAN, BUT CHILDREN MAKE HIM NERVOUS!
©
SCHULZ

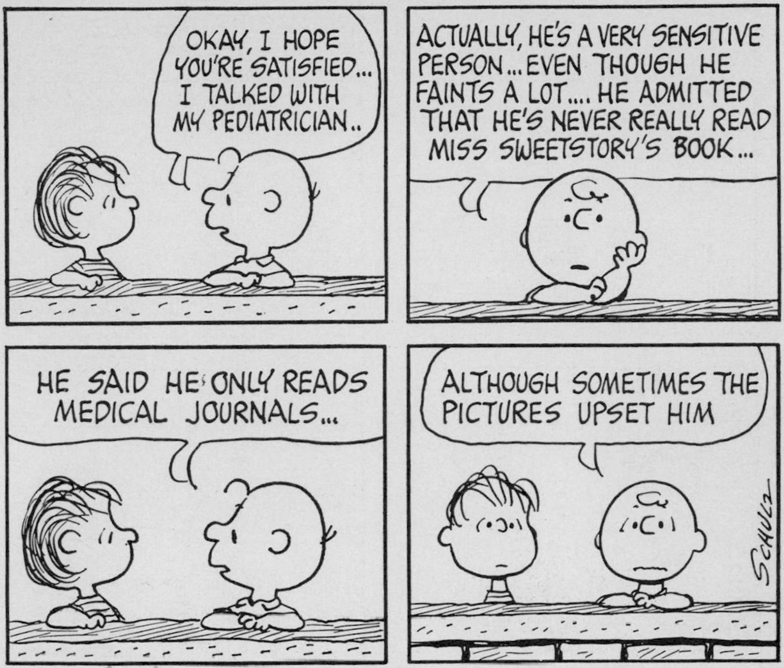
OKAY, I HOPE YOU'RE SATISFIED... I TALKED WITH MY PEDIATRICIAN..
ACTUALLY, HE'S A VERY SENSITIVE PERSON...EVEN THOUGH HE FAINTS A LOT.... HE ADMITTED THAT HE'S NEVER REALLY READ MISS SWEETSTORY'S BOOK...
HE SAID HE ONLY READS MEDICAL JOURNALS...
ALTHOUGH SOMETIMES THE PICTURES UPSET HIM
SCHULZ

I'M AWAKE!!
SCHULZ

PEPPERMINT PATTY LOVES
LIFE IS LIKE A BRACELET, CHUCK
LIKE A WHAT?
LIFE IS LIKE A BRACELET... IT HAS LITTLE JEWELS AROUND IT WHICH ARE LIKE THE LITTLE BRIGHT MOMENTS THAT COME ALONG IN OUR LIVES EVERY NOW AND THEN...
DO YOU FEEL THAT THIS HAS BEEN ONE OF THOSE BRIGHT MOMENTS, CHUCK? DO YOU FEEL THAT THIS HOUR WE HAVE HAD TOGETHER HAS BEEN LIKE A DIAMOND SET IN A BRACELET?
DO YOU FEEL THAT WAY, CHUCK? IF YOU DO, YOU SHOULD TELL ME..
WHY, YES...I THINK YOU'RE RIGHT.. LIFE IS VERY MUCH LIKE A COLLAR..
NOT A COLLAR, CHUCK.. A BRACELET!!!
SPEAKING OF COLLARS, SWEETIE.. I'M AN EXPERT!
I REMEMBER ONCE BACK ABOUT FIVE YEARS AGO... I SAID THE RIGHT THING..
SCHULZ

ROSEBUD!
IS THERE A LOT OF SWEARING IN THIS MOVIE ?
I DON'T WANT TO SEE IT IF THERE'S A LOT OF SWEARING.. I'M NOT IN THE ARMY, YOU KNOW!
I LIKE TO THINK OF MYSELF AS A LADY, AND I REFUSE TO GO TO A MOVIE THAT HAS A LOT OF SWEARING...
WHY DO YOU TAKE ME TO MOVIES THAT HAVE A LOT OF SWEARING?
I'M NOT TAKING YOU TO THE MOVIES
WE'RE STANDING IN LINE TOGETHER, AREN'T WE ?
THAT DOESN'T MEAN I'M TAKING YOU !
I GUESS IT DOESN'T, DOES IT ? *SIGH*
ONE, PLEASE
FORGET IT !
WHAT ARE YOU DOING HOME ? I THOUGHT YOU WENT TO THE MOVIES...
I AM... I'M WATCHING "CITIZEN KANE" FOR THE TENTH TIME !
SCHULZ

?
SIGH
I HATE PLAYING "BAT"!

?
THERE ARE A LOT OF THINGS IN THIS WORLD THAT WOODSTOCK HAS NEVER SEEN...ONE OF THEM IS A SALT LICK!

flitter
HI, FEATHERS!
WOODSTOCK JUST HATES TO BE CALLED "FEATHERS"
!
HEE HEE HEE HEE HEE!
BANANA NOSE?!
HEE HEE HEE HEE HEE HEE
!
I GUESS IT'S BEST TO COME OUT EVEN...
SCHULZ

SOME MORNING I'M GOING TO GET UP REAL EARLY, AND WATCH THE SUN RISE...
ACTUALLY, AS YOU PROBABLY KNOW, THE SUN DOESN'T RISE.. THE EARTH TURNS...
SOME MORNING I'M GOING TO GET UP REAL EARLY, AND WATCH THE EARTH TURN...
SCHULZ

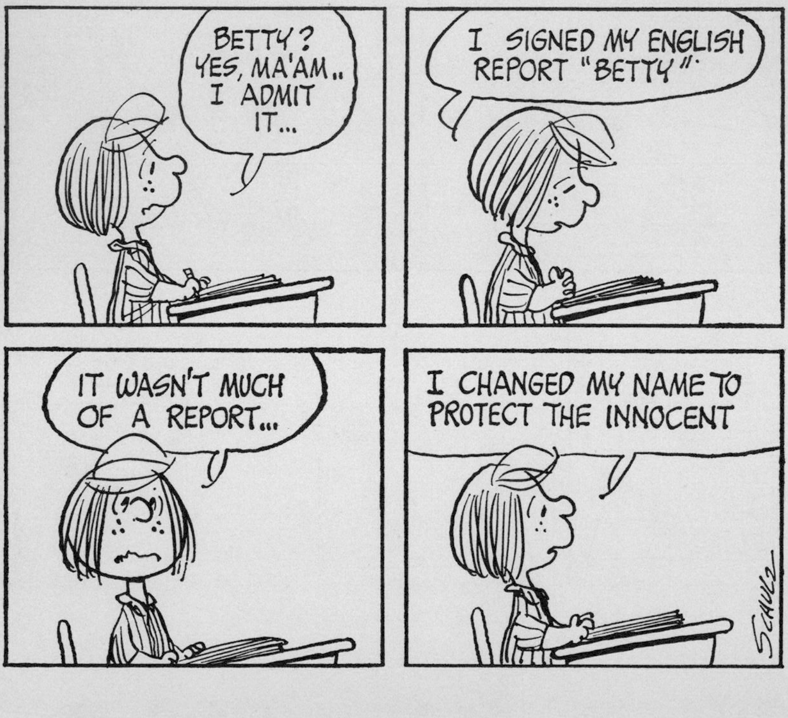
BETTY? YES, MA'AM.. I ADMIT IT...
I SIGNED MY ENGLISH REPORT "BETTY"
IT WASN'T MUCH OF A REPORT...
I CHANGED MY NAME TO PROTECT THE INNOCENT
SCHULZ

AH! A LETTER FROM MY PUBLISHER!
HMM..
Author Questionnaire; These questions are designed to prepare the media with information.
Author's name Snoopy
Residence Just a doghouse.
Phone unlisted
Birth See records at Daisy Hill Puppy Farm.
Citizenship Papers misplaced. These things happen.
Reason for writing Book I wrote from a sense of need. I needed something to do. You can't just sleep all day long.
I was one of eight Beagles. We had a happy life. Lots to eat and a good cage, although looking out at the world through chicken wire can get to you after awhile.
Married Almost once, but that's a long story.
Schools and Colleges attended Obedience School dropout.
Suggestions for Promotion If you don't promote my book, I'll get another publisher so fast it will make your head spin.
I LIKE FILLING OUT QUESTIONNAIRES!
SCHULZ

IT'S MIGRATING TIME...
THIS IS THE TIME OF YEAR WHEN MILLIONS OF BIRDS ARE TAKING OFF FOR WARMER CLIMATES...
ALL BUT WOODSTOCK, WHO'S AFRAID OF GETTING MUGGED!
SIGH
SCHULZ

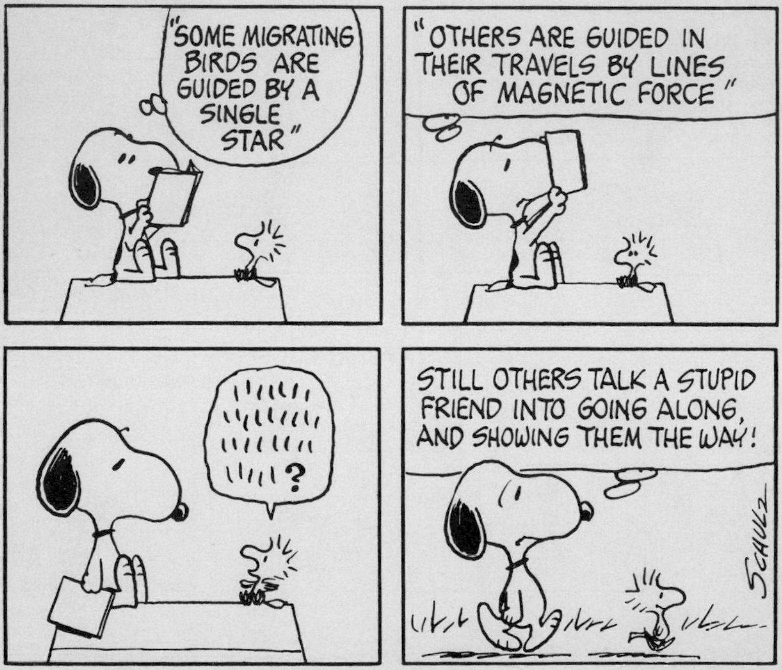
"SOME MIGRATING BIRDS ARE GUIDED BY A SINGLE STAR"
"OTHERS ARE GUIDED IN THEIR TRAVELS BY LINES OF MAGNETIC FORCE"
?
STILL OTHERS TALK A STUPID FRIEND INTO GOING ALONG, AND SHOWING THEM THE WAY!
SCHULZ

WHERE IN THE WORLD ARE THEY GOING?
I THINK THEY'RE MIGRATING
BEAGLES DON'T MIGRATE!
HEY, STUPID, HASN'T ANYONE EVER TOLD YOU BEAGLES DON'T MIGRATE?
I HATE BEING MOCKED BY LOW TYPES!
SCHULZ

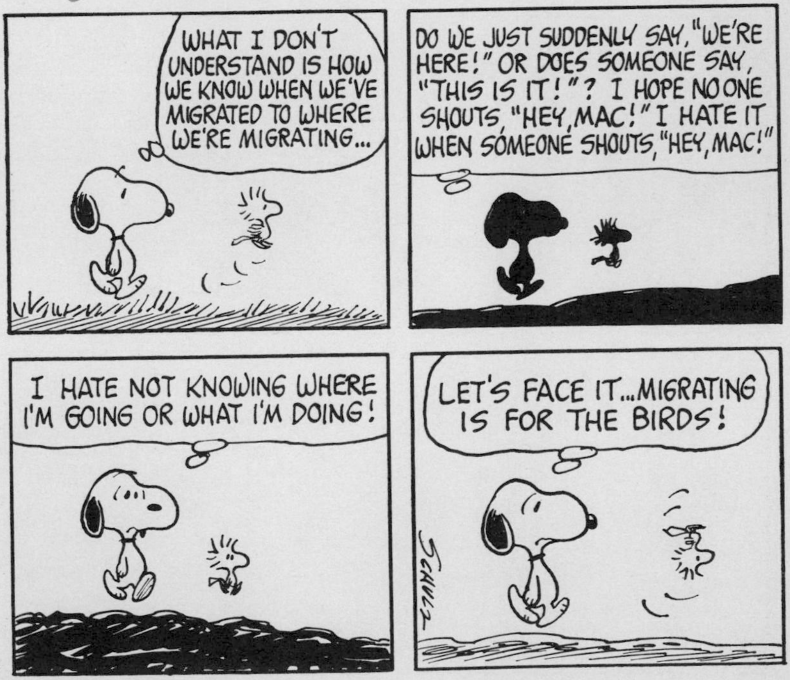
WHAT I DON'T UNDERSTAND IS HOW WE KNOW WHEN WE'VE MIGRATED TO WHERE WE'RE MIGRATING...
DO WE JUST SUDDENLY SAY, "WE'RE HERE!" OR DOES SOMEONE SAY, "THIS IS IT!"? I HOPE NO ONE SHOUTS, "HEY, MAC!" I HATE IT WHEN SOMEONE SHOUTS, "HEY, MAC!"
I HATE NOT KNOWING WHERE I'M GOING OR WHAT I'M DOING!
SCHULZ
LET'S FACE IT...MIGRATING IS FOR THE BIRDS!

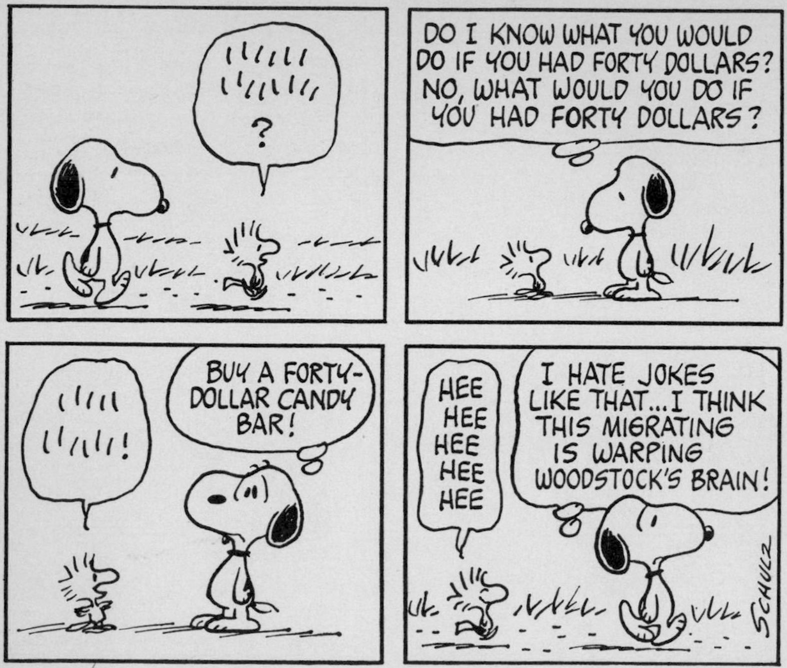

DO I KNOW WHAT YOU WOULD DO IF YOU HAD FORTY DOLLARS? NO, WHAT WOULD YOU DO IF YOU HAD FORTY DOLLARS?
BUY A FORTY-DOLLAR CANDY BAR!
HEE HEE HEE HEE HEE
I HATE JOKES LIKE THAT... I THINK THIS MIGRATING IS WARPING WOODSTOCK'S BRAIN!
SCHULZ

OKAY, FRIEND, THIS IS AS FAR AS I GO...
YOU CAN SORT OF MIGRATE HERE FOR THE WINTER... HAVE A GOOD TIME... I'LL SEE YOU IN THE SPRING...
I KNEW THIS WOULD HAPPEN!
SCHULZ

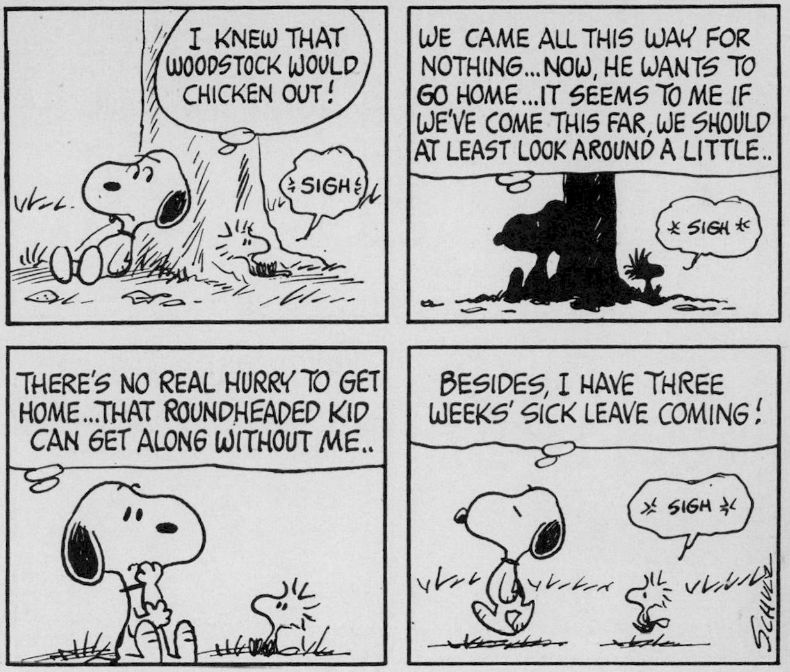
I KNEW THAT WOODSTOCK WOULD CHICKEN OUT!
SIGH
WE CAME ALL THIS WAY FOR NOTHING...NOW, HE WANTS TO GO HOME...IT SEEMS TO ME IF WE'VE COME THIS FAR, WE SHOULD AT LEAST LOOK AROUND A LITTLE..
SIGH
THERE'S NO REAL HURRY TO GET HOME...THAT ROUNDHEADED KID CAN GET ALONG WITHOUT ME..
BESIDES, I HAVE THREE WEEKS' SICK LEAVE COMING!
SIGH
SCHULZ

YOU KNOW WHERE WE ARE? WE'RE NEAR THE DAISY HILL PUPPY FARM!
I CAN SHOW WOODSTOCK WHERE I WAS BORN! WOW!! THIS IS GREAT! WHAT A THRILL THIS WILL BE FOR WOODSTOCK!
I CAN SHOW HIM MY OLD CAGE, AND WHERE WE ATE, AND WHERE WE PLAYED AND EVERYTHING!
WOODSTOCK WILL BE SO EXCITED!
YAWN!
SCHULZ

IT'S GONE!! THE DAISY HILL PUPPY FARM IS GONE!
THEY'VE BUILT A SIX-STORY PARKING GARAGE! AAUGH! I CAN'T STAND IT!!
?
YOU STUPID PEOPLE!!
YOU'RE PARKING ON MY MEMORIES!!!

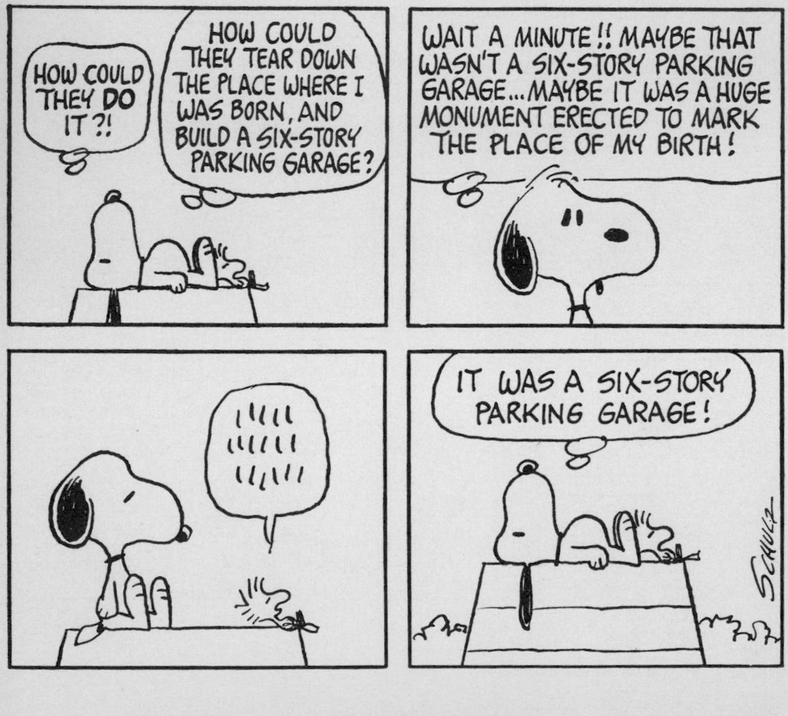
HOW COULD THEY DO IT?!
HOW COULD THEY TEAR DOWN THE PLACE WHERE I WAS BORN, AND BUILD A SIX-STORY PARKING GARAGE?
WAIT A MINUTE!! MAYBE THAT WASN'T A SIX-STORY PARKING GARAGE...MAYBE IT WAS A HUGE MONUMENT ERECTED TO MARK THE PLACE OF MY BIRTH!
IT WAS A SIX-STORY PARKING GARAGE!

Pay to the Order of Me!
money, money, money $ and more money
Linus Van Pelt
HA!! LOOK AT THAT!
IT'S STARTING TO SNOW, AND I'M READY!
I'M GOING TO BE THE FIRST KID IN THE NEIGHBORHOOD TO SHOVEL WALKS..
I'M GOING FROM HOUSE TO HOUSE, AND I'M GOING TO SHOVEL EVERY SIDEWALK AND DRIVEWAY THAT I CAN FIND!
WILL YOU MAKE A LOT OF MONEY?
YOU BET I'LL MAKE A LOT OF MONEY! AND YOU THINK I'LL SPEND IT RIGHT AWAY, DON'T YOU? WELL, I WON'T!
I'LL PROBABLY PUT IT ALL IN A SAVINGS ACCOUNT, AND JUST LIVE OFF THE INTEREST, OR MAYBE I'LL BUY AN ANNUITY PAYABLE AT AGE TWELVE, OR MAYBE I'LL INVEST IT ALL IN SOME MUTUAL FUNDS, OR EVEN BUY SOME STOCK IN ONE OF OUR LOCAL COMPANIES THAT SEEMS TO BE GETTING BIGGER, OR...
..OR MAYBE I'LL... I'LL...
I REMEMBER READING ABOUT ABRAHAM LINCOLN, AND HOW HE USED TO DO HIS HOMEWORK WITH A PIECE OF COAL ON THE BACK OF A SHOVEL...
FORGET IT!
SCHULZ

FOR "SHOW AND TELL" TODAY, I HAVE A LITTLE SURPRISE...
I HAVE BROUGHT THE FIRST SNOWFLAKE OF THE YEAR! NOW, AS YOU MAY OR MAY NOT KNOW, SNOWFLAKES ARE...
DUE TO CIRCUMSTANCES BEYOND OUR CONTROL, THIS PORTION OF "SHOW AND TELL" HAS BEEN CANCELLED!
SCHULZ

I THINK IT WOULD BE VERY ROMANTIC IF SOMEDAY YOU GAVE ME A SINGLE PERFECT ROSE
OR A CARNATION...OR EVEN AN OLD DANDELION...
HOW ABOUT A HANDFUL OF CRAB GRASS?
I'LL TAKE IT!
SCHULZ

STUPID KID!
PSYCHIATRIC HELP 7¢
DREAMS SERVE A VERY USEFUL PURPOSE...
THE DOCTOR IS IN
PSYCHIATRIC HELP 7¢
THE DREAMS OF NIGHT PREPARE YOU FOR THE DAY THAT FOLLOWS..
THE DOCTOR IS IN
HELP
WHAT DOES THAT MEAN?
THE DOCTOR IS IN
IT'S AT NIGHT, CHARLIE BROWN, WHEN YOU'RE SLEEPING, THAT YOUR BRAIN IS REALLY WORKING...
THE DOCTOR IS IN
YOUR BRAIN IS TRYING TO SORT EVERYTHING OUT FOR YOU...
THE DOCTOR
IT'S TRYING TO MAKE YOU SEE YOURSELF AS YOU REALLY ARE..
THE DOCTOR
PSYCHIATRIC HELP 7¢
EVEN MY BRAIN IS AGAINST ME!
THE DOCTOR IS IN
SCHULZ

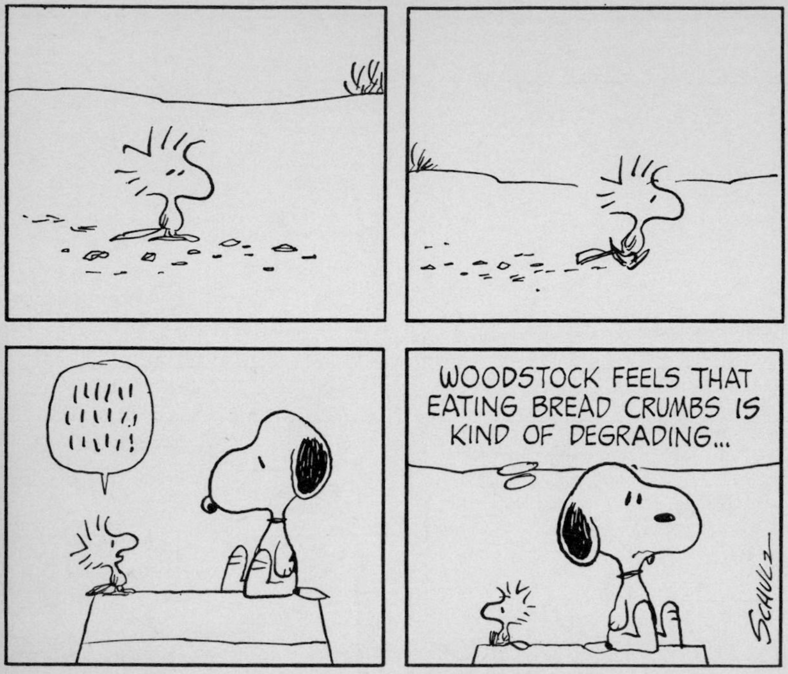
WOODSTOCK FEELS THAT EATING BREAD CRUMBS IS KIND OF DEGRADING...
SCHULZ

WOODSTOCK THINKS THAT IF YOU SIT IN A MAILBOX LONG ENOUGH, YOU'LL GET A CHRISTMAS CARD...HE'S SO NAIVE...HE JUST..
SCHULZ

English Theme
"The True Meaning of Christmas."
To me, Christmas is the joy of getting.
YOU MEAN 'GIVING'... CHRISTMAS IS THE JOY OF GIVING....
I DON'T HAVE THE SLIGHTEST IDEA WHAT YOU'RE TALKING ABOUT!
SCHULZ

Christmas is getting all you can get while the getting is good.
GIVING! THE ONLY REAL JOY IS GIVING!
LIKE, WOW!
SCHULZ

LET'S SEE NOW... HOW CAN I PUT THIS INTO WORDS?
WHAT I MEAN IS... WHAT I WANT TO SAY IS... HOW CAN I PUT IT INTO WORDS? WHAT I'M TRYING TO SAY IS...
POW!
RATS! I WAS HOPING SHE COULD PUT IT INTO WORDS...
SCHULZ

YOU HIT ME YESTERDAY, REMEMBER?
THEREFORE, I'VE DECIDED NOT TO GET YOU ANYTHING FOR CHRISTMAS THIS YEAR!
WHAT ARE YOU DOING??
TAKING BACK A HIT!
SCHULZ

YOU HAVE TO GIVE ME A CHRISTMAS PRESENT!
THAT'S THE CHRISTMAS RULE!! YOU CAN'T IGNORE THE CHRISTMAS RULE!!
I CAN DO ANYTHING I WANT! YOU HIT ME SO I'VE DECIDED NOT TO GIVE YOU ANYTHING FOR CHRISTMAS!
I MAY HAVE TO SUFFER MARTYRDOM...
SCHULZ

YOU HAVE TO GIVE ME A CHRISTMAS PRESENT! IT SAYS SO IN THE BIBLE!
YOU'RE BLUFFING...THE BIBLE SAYS NOTHING ABOUT GIVING CHRISTMAS PRESENTS!
IT DOESN'T?
YOU CAN'T BLUFF AN OLD THEOLOGIAN!
SCHULZ
* SIGH *

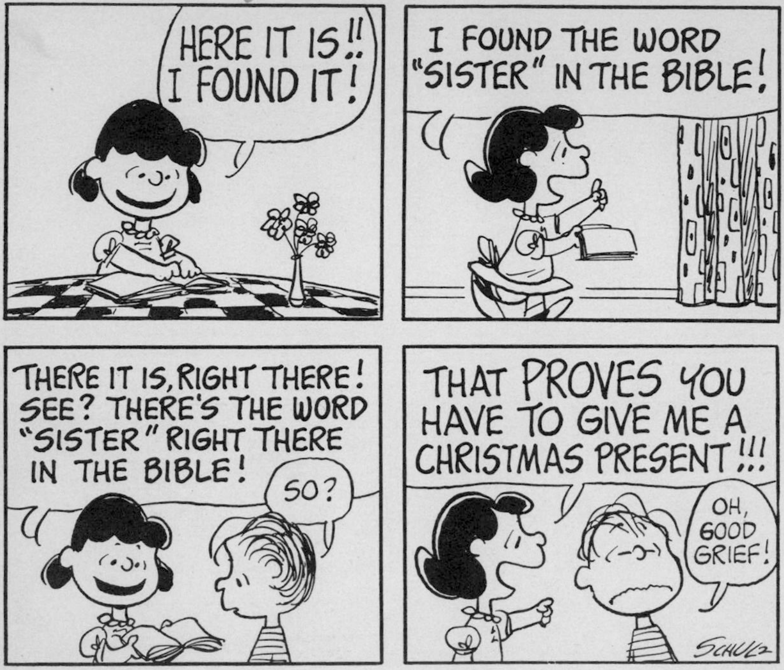
HERE IT IS!! I FOUND IT!
I FOUND THE WORD "SISTER" IN THE BIBLE!
THERE IT IS, RIGHT THERE! SEE? THERE'S THE WORD "SISTER" RIGHT THERE IN THE BIBLE!
SO?
THAT PROVES YOU HAVE TO GIVE ME A CHRISTMAS PRESENT!!!
OH, GOOD GRIEF!
SCHULZ

SO YOU FOUND THE WORD "SISTER" IN THE BIBLE...
WHAT DOES **THAT** PROVE?
IT PROVES I KNOW MORE ABOUT THE BIBLE THAN YOU THOUGHT!
DID YOU FIND IT IN THE OLD TESTAMENT OR IN THE NEW TESTAMENT?
THE WHAT?
AH, HA!
I MAY HAVE TO HIT HIM AGAIN!
SCHULZ

Season's Greetings
I'LL READ THE LIST, AND YOU CAN TELL ME WHAT YOU WANT TO DO..
DO YOU WANT TO SEND A CHRISTMAS CARD TO MILLIE?
NO, LET'S FORGET MILLIE... I DON'T THINK SHE REALLY LIKES ME..
HOW ABOUT THE O'HARAS?
I DON'T KNOW... IT'S KIND OF HARD TO DECIDE...
THERE'S TINA... HOW ABOUT TINA?
TINA LIKES ME, BUT I DON'T KNOW...
HOW ABOUT JANET?
WELL, MAYBE...
I KNOW YOU DON'T WANT TO SEND A CARD TO 'POOCHIE'
I'M GLAD YOU KNOW THAT!
KIM? RANDI? NORMA?
NOPE! NOPE! NOPE!
HOW ABOUT AMY? I THINK AMY SHOULD GET A CARD
MAYBE YOU'RE RIGHT
OKAY, IT'S SETTLED.. YOU'LL SEND A CARD TO AMY... I'LL MAIL IT OUT TODAY...
THANK YOU
THAT'S THE TROUBLE WITH HAVING ONLY ONE STAMP...
SCHULZ

MY REPORT TODAY IS ON DINOSAURS...
THE LARGEST DINOSAUR THAT EVER LIVED WAS THE BRONCHITIS
IT SOON BECAME EXTINCT...
IT COUGHED A LOT!
SCHULZ

Ten milligrams equals one centigram.
Ten decigrams equals one gram.
Ten grams equals one grampa.
KEEP GOING... I CAN HARDLY WAIT TO SEE WHAT COMES NEXT...
SCHULZ

PSYCHIATRIC HELP 7¢
THE DOCTOR IS IN
I KNOW I NEED HELP... I DON'T DENY THAT..
..BUT SOMEHOW I FEEL THAT I DON'T REALLY WANT TO GO THROUGH THE WHOLE PSYCHIATRIC BIT...YOU KNOW WHAT I MEAN?
ABSOLUTELY...JUST STEP OVER HERE, PLEASE...
GOOD, SOUND, MOTHERLY ADVICE
MOM IS IN
SCHULZ

HAPPY BEETHOVEN'S BIRTHDAY! AREN'T YOU GOING TO KISS ME?
GOOD GRIEF, NO!!
BEETHOVEN WOULD HAVE WANTED YOU TO!
I DOUBT THAT VERY MUCH!
WELL, I'LL BET BRAHMS WOULD HAVE WANTED YOU TO!!
SCHULZ

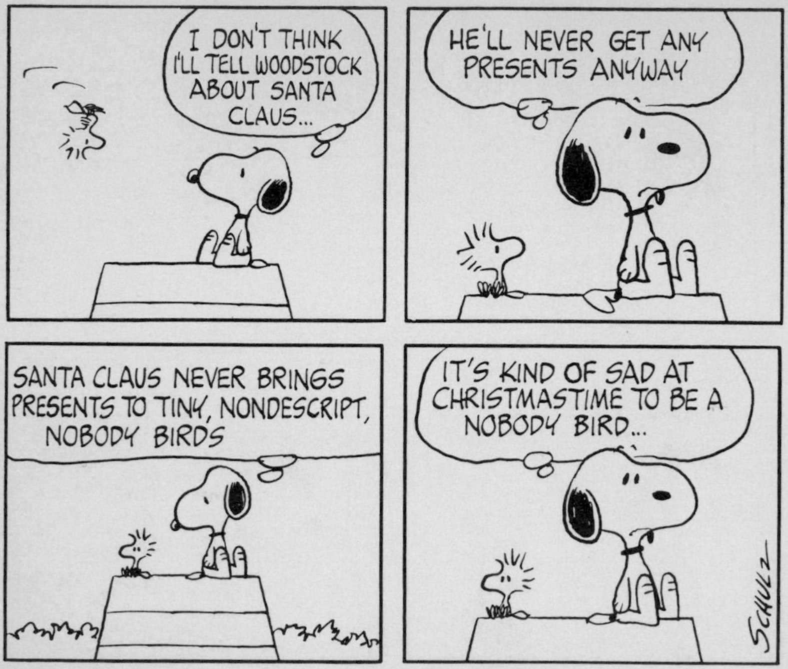
I DON'T THINK I'LL TELL WOODSTOCK ABOUT SANTA CLAUS...
HE'LL NEVER GET ANY PRESENTS ANYWAY
SANTA CLAUS NEVER BRINGS PRESENTS TO TINY, NONDESCRIPT, NOBODY BIRDS
IT'S KIND OF SAD AT CHRISTMASTIME TO BE A NOBODY BIRD...
SCHULZ

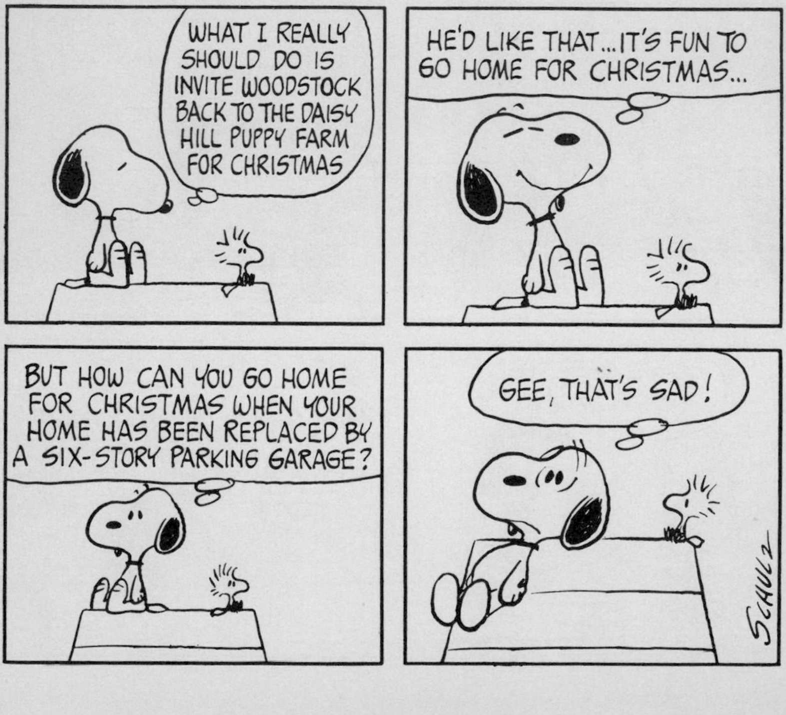
WHAT I REALLY SHOULD DO IS INVITE WOODSTOCK BACK TO THE DAISY HILL PUPPY FARM FOR CHRISTMAS
HE'D LIKE THAT...IT'S FUN TO GO HOME FOR CHRISTMAS...
BUT HOW CAN YOU GO HOME FOR CHRISTMAS WHEN YOUR HOME HAS BEEN REPLACED BY A SIX-STORY PARKING GARAGE?
GEE, THAT'S SAD!
SCHULZ

Z
POOCHIE ?!
GUESS WHAT! YOU GOT A CHRISTMAS CARD FROM POOCHIE!
OH, NO!!
I'LL BET YOU DIDN'T SEND HER ONE, DID YOU?
OF COURSE, I DIDN'T... I WOULDN'T SEND POOCHIE A ROCK!
SHE WROTE A LITTLE NOTE ON THE BACK OF THE CARD...
I DON'T WANT TO HEAR IT!
"DEAR SNOOPY, I HOPE YOU HAVE A NICE CHRISTMAS...I THINK I AM GOING TO BE OUT YOUR WAY SOON...I'LL TRY TO STOP BY...SAY HELLO TO CHARLIE BROWN"
IF SHE COMES WITHIN A THOUSAND MILES OF ME, I'LL SCREAM!
IT'LL BE KIND OF NICE TO SEE POOCHIE AGAIN
SEEING POOCHIE AGAIN WOULD BE LIKE GETTING THE MUMPS TWICE!
YOU'VE NEVER FORGIVEN HER HAVE YOU?
YOU DON'T FORGIVE SOMEONE WHO DOES TO YOU WHAT SHE DID TO ME!
ANYWAY, HERE'S THE CARD..
I'LL BET SHE DOESN'T EVEN REMEMBER WHAT HAPPENED..
THAT WOULD BE JUST LIKE HER NOT TO REMEMBER...SHE'LL COME TO SEE ME, TOO... I KNOW SHE WILL..
JUST WHAT I DIDN'T NEED... A POOCHIE CHRISTMAS!
SCHULZ

POOCHIE'S HERE! SHE WANTS TO SEE YOU
I DON'T WANT TO SEE HER ...NOT AFTER WHAT SHE DID TO ME..
THAT WAS A LONG TIME AGO..
I DON'T CARE... WE BEAGLES HAVE MEMORIES LIKE BEAGLES!
"THERE I WAS, AN INNOCENT LITTLE PUPPY, BOUNCING AROUND THE YARD ONE DAY...EAGER TO PLEASE..WILLING TO DO ANYTHING FOR A LITTLE AFFECTION..."
"THEN THIS LITTLE GIRL COMES ALONG...'POOCHIE' WAS HER NAME..SHE HAD A STICK IN HER HAND"
"'HI, CUTE PUPPY!' SHE SAYS. 'DO YOU WANT TO CHASE THE STICK?'"
"SO SHE THROWS THE STICK, AND I, LIKE A FOOL, GO RUNNING AFTER IT..."
"...FALLING ALL OVER MYSELF, BUMPING MY NOSE AND GETTING A MOUTHFUL OF MUD..."
"I GO RUNNING BACK WITH THE STICK, BRIGHT AND EAGER.."
"..JUST IN TIME TO SEE HER WALKING AWAY WITH AN ENGLISH SHEEP DOG!"
I'M AMAZED THAT YOU REMEMBER ALL THAT
HOW COULD I FORGET?
I STILL HAVE THE STICK!
SCHULZ

WHY COULDN'T SHE JUST STAY AWAY ?
WHY DID SHE HAVE TO COME BACK ?
POOCHIE, IT'S GOOD TO SEE YOU AFTER ALL THESE YEARS..
WHERE'S SNOOPY ?
YOU WERE THE ONE WHO FIRST STARTED TO CALL ME CHARLIE BROWN ...
I WONDER IF SNOOPY WILL REMEMBER ME...
HE'S CHANGED A LITTLE SINCE YOU LIVED AROUND HERE...
HE'S PROBABLY OUT IN THE BACK YARD AND...
I'M REALLY ANXIOUS TO SEE HIM ... I REMEMBER WHAT A CUTE LITTLE PUPPY HE WAS...
SNOOPY ?
SNOOPY, WHERE ARE YOU ? SNOOPY ?
!
THOMAS WOLFE WAS RIGHT... YOU CAN'T GO HOME AGAIN !

I LOVE THE HOLIDAY SEASON!
I LIKE TO SEE PEOPLE BUYING PRESENTS AND DECORATING THEIR HOMES...I LIKE CHRISTMAS TREES, TOO
EVERYONE SHOULD HAVE A CHRISTMAS TREE... EVEN WOODSTOCK..
SCHULZ

IT SNOWED LAST NIGHT..
NOW, I CAN'T SEE A THING... SUDDENLY I'M SHUT OFF FROM THE WORLD AND ALL ITS PROBLEMS
LET'S HEAR IT FOR THE SNOW!!
SCHULZ

I JUST WANTED TO THANK YOU AGAIN FOR THE STRING OF PEARLS YOU GAVE ME FOR CHRISTMAS...
I DID NOT GIVE YOU A STRING OF PEARLS FOR CHRISTMAS..
I'LL SAY YOU DIDN'T!
SCHULZ

RING!
HI! I JUST STOPPED BY TO THANK YOU AGAIN FOR THE MINK STOLE YOU GAVE ME FOR CHRISTMAS
I DID NOT GIVE YOU A MINK STOLE FOR CHRISTMAS!
I'LL SAY YOU DIDN'T!
SCHULZ

I HATE TO SAY THIS, BUT YOU'VE BEEN VERY CRABBY SINCE CHRISTMAS
ANYONE WHO IS AT ALL SENSITIVE IS BOUND TO HAVE A POST-CHRISTMAS LETDOWN!
ISN'T BEING CRABBY AND HAVING A POST-CHRISTMAS LETDOWN REALLY THE SAME THING?
NOT AT ALL!!
SCHULZ

SHE MAY HAVE HONKED, BUT I NEVER HEARD HER!
SCHULZ

THIS IS SOME TEST
"WHO WAS CYRIL FOX? DISCUSS BRIEFLY THE BRONZE AGE"
"WHO WERE THE BEAKER PEOPLE? WHO WAS CASSIVELLAUNUS? WHO WAS CUNOBELIN? WHAT WERE THE CAUSEWAYED CAMPS?"
IT'S GUESSING TIME!
SCHULZ

WHAT DID YOU GET ON THE TEST, PATTY?
I GOT A "D MINUS"
THAT'S TOO BAD
IT DOESN'T BOTHER ME...
I'M JUST GLAD I HAVE MY HEALTH!
SCHULZ

TRUE
FALSE
!!
?
QUESTION NUMBER ONE...
TRUE!
TRUE AGAIN! FALSE!
TRUE, BY GOLLY! AND FALSE AND TRUE AND TRUE!
FALSE AGAIN!! THERE'S NO DOUBT ABOUT IT!
TRUE! THAT ONE IS ABSOLUTELY TRUE!
FALSE! FALSE! FALSE! TRUE!
OH, I SAY THIS ONE IS REALLY FALSE!!
TRUE! FALSE! TRUE! FALSE! TRUE! FALSE!
TRUE, BY GOLLY! TRUE!!
PSST! PATTY!
HUH? WHAT? WHAT'S THE MATTER? HUH?
YOU WERE GETTING KIND OF LOUD..
HOW EMBARRASSING
IT'S EASY TO GET CARRIED AWAY IN THESE TRUE OR FALSE TESTS...
SCHULZ

YOU ONLY EAT THE CENTER OF YOUR BREAD?
THAT'S THE PART I LIKE
WHAT DO YOU DO WITH THE REST OF IT?
THROW IT TO THE BIRDS...
SCHULZ

DO YOU THINK THERE ARE OTHER PEOPLE IN OUTER SPACE?
NO! ABSOLUTELY NOT!
IF THERE WERE, THEY MOST CERTAINLY WOULD HAVE TRIED TO CONTACT ME!
THAT SETTLES THAT!
SCHULZ

DO YOU WANT TO TAKE ME TO THE SENIOR PROM?
THAT WON'T BE FOR ANOTHER TEN YEARS
I JUST WANTED TO GIVE YOU A BREAK...IN TEN YEARS I PLAN TO BE THE MOST SOUGHT-AFTER GIRL IN SCHOOL!
I HAVE NO INTENTION TO SEEK AFTER YOU..
WELL, IF YOU DO, I'LL BE STANDING BY THE DRINKING FOUNTAIN AT THE NORTH END OF THE BUILDING!!
THERE'S NO SENSE TO BEING SOUGHT AFTER IF YOU CAN'T BE FOUND!
SCHULZ